KARL LEW

COOL MAN LEWK

MY JOURNEY FROM
ORPHAN TO CRIMEFIGHTER

a memoir

DEDICATION

I dedicate this book of my lifetime's worth of memories to my beloved late wife, Toni, and our loving family.

Dear Toni,

It was August 1956 when we met at the Lake County Fair. We spent our first Christmas together that December. My first and my finest memories are of that time. Our last Christmas together was December 2015; we were blessed to share fifty-nine Christmases together. My first Christmas without you is 2016. We all miss you—Bob and Connie, Bobbie, Bonnie, Dakota, Gracie, Ellie, Coleton, Justin and Mike.

I think of you now as an angel of God, and I believe that you've been blessed by God to spend Christmas together with your entire family. Our time together on Earth was the best I could ever hope for. You have been my life's best friend, partner, wife, and mother to our children. God truly blessed us and blessed me in a special way by giving you to me. How generous God was to me because, without you, I would have been nothing. Your family has been the only family I'd had since meeting you.

It must be incredibly beautiful in heaven at Christmastime. I can visualize you with your beloved family, your dad and mom, Don, Terry, Janice, Bonnie, Bud, and Peanut, who is the latest to die. What a blessed reunion. I am so happy for you, although I miss you dearly; you are free of pain and suffering. I love you and miss you. You will always be my one and only love on this Earth. Goodbye for now. I hope you love our book.

Love, Karl.

CHAPTER ONE

THE EARLY YEARS

I WAS BORN ON OCTOBER 13, 1940 and was the first of four children. My mother, Irma, was a second-generation Italian and was just seventeen years old. My father, Karl, was of Polish descent and was twenty years old; both parents were raised Roman Catholic. I was followed by my brother Tony (1943) and two younger sisters, Carol (1944) and Linda (1945).

Cleveland, Ohio, was booming during the war years due to its many manufacturing plants. Jobs were plentiful, but Karl had difficulty holding a job. The following quotes from Cuyahoga County Child Welfare documents best describe life in our household:

"During their marriage, the children did not receive proper care or supervision in their home. There was much drinking followed by violent, abusive behavior by the father. There was also considerable hostility to relatives because one side was Polish and the other was Italian. The children were undernourished, and the home was one of filth and neglect."

Our father was unstable, immature and an alcoholic. Although he made many promises to amend his ways, he always failed to do so. The welfare documents describe him thus:

"[Mr. Lewkowski] had an extremely poor work record and many contacts with the courts. On October 28, 1947, he was picked up by the East Cleveland Police on a petty larceny charge. The following month he was picked up by East Cleveland Police for starting a fight in a saloon and was given thirty days in the workhouse. Upon his release, he continued drinking and created many unpleasant scenes in his mother's home and boarding houses. He frequently took the children out to beer parlors and kept them there for hours. He often arrived drunk and started quarreling with the children and beating them. He had served sentences in the Warrensville Workhouse for non-support, drunkenness, bond forfeiture, escape from workhouse, and neglect of children."

My mother was described as "quite immature and incapable of giving the children adequate care."

Our "bedrooms" were small cubicles with curtains as doorways. It is funny how some childhood memories are vivid and others not so. My brother Tony and I recall going alone to the movies in a neighborhood theater. We saw a movie called *The Beast with Five Fingers* in 1946, and we sat in the front row. Tony remembers how scared he was watching that hand play the piano.

Tony says a stranger with a red convertible found us wandering in front of the theater after the movie and took us home. He still remembers the scene where the severed hand played the piano while he hunkered down in his seat.

I recall being in the beer parlors with my father and going up and down the bar drinking what was left in some of the glasses. There were times we slept at the bars into the night. One night my father and I came home late, and my mother was terribly upset. She locked us both out of the apartment, and my father and I slept rough that night. I was six years old.

I also have some slightly better memories of my father; I remember staying in hotels with him and having dinner with him late in the evening. Later, he would play on the bed with me and make me laugh. Later in life, I learned my father had been judged by the court system as being incorrigible. He spent time in the workhouse, but he escaped several times and would drink and get involved in fights. He was also on probation for petty larceny. The only mementos my brother and I have from him are two little Catholic prayer books, which we both still have today.

In 1946, when I was six, Karl and Irma divorced. My father went his separate way, leaving the rest of us to survive on public assistance (now known as welfare). The following year, in 1947, our mother died in a tragic accident. She and her younger sister, Velma, were sunbathing on the roof of the tenement building where we lived. Velma had walked across the skylight safely, but when Irma followed her, the glass broke. After spending weeks in a coma, my mother died. I was six years old at the time of the accident. I have a vague memory of the sound of broken glass and screams as she fell. Shortly after her death, we four kids became wards of Cuyahoga County.

A 24 year old East Side woman, mother of four children, was injured critically yesterday afternoon when she fell through a skylight on the roof of her apartment building where she and two companions had gone to sun bathe.

The victim was Mrs. Irma Lewkowski. 10121 Barret Avenue N. E.

Preceding Mrs. Lewkowski across the glass skylight of the two-story building were her sister Miss Velma D'Errico, 17, of 10401 Barret Avenue, and Miss LaVerne Howells, 18, of 382 E. 105th Street. The three-by-six skylight was above an open stairwell.

Police estimate Mrs. Lewkowski's fall at about 30 feet. She was taken by police to Glenville hospital, where she was said to have internal injuries.

Mrs. Lewkowski, a divorcee, has four children ranging in age from 2 to 6 years. Two of the children were asleep at the time of the accident.

Skylight Breaks; Sun Bather Hurt

MRS. IRMA LEWKOWSKI

**Clevland Plain Dealer
June 29, 1947**

Carol and Linda, the two youngest children, went into the foster care/adoption system. I can barely remember what they were like when they were babies. My brother and I were sent to stay with our paternal grandmother, Mrs. Mayou, a widow who lived at 324 E. 26th St. in Willowick, Ohio. That was the last we saw of our little sisters until many years later, when we were all adults. More on that a little later.

After our mother's death, our father lived in Michigan and several other places. Years later, on June 14, 1957, at age thirty-eight, he died of a heart attack in Erie, Pennsylvania. He had been in poor health for about two years, probably because of his heavy drinking.

My brother and I slept in the same bed at Grandma Mayou's, falling asleep with our arms wrapped around each other. I do not remember being abused or being hungry at any time while we were there, nor do I recall my father ever being with us.

THE ORPHANAGE

One day our social worker showed up and told us that Grandma Mayou was no longer able to care for us. She loaded us and our meager belongings into her car and drove us to an orphanage called Parmadale. I remember looking through the rear window of the car and seeing our grandmother standing in the street, crying and waving at us as we were driven away. My brother and I were both confused, afraid, and crying. We had no idea where we were going. It was not that long ago, after all, that we had been taken this same way after our mother died. Where were our sisters? Where was our father? Why could we not stay with Grandma?

No one had any answers to those questions, of course. Ultimately, Tony and I would live at the

Parmadale Cottage

orphanage for about four and a half years before our discharge in September 1952.

Cleveland historical documents describe Parmadale's design as "a surrounding as nearly like home as possible. The children, varying in size and age, are lodged in cottages under the motherly care of the sisters. The plan also provided opportunity for brothers of different ages to live together."

It was April 16, 1948, when we entered Parmadale. Tony was almost five years old and I was seven. The orphanage was a beautiful place, with its own school and plenty of recreational facilities. Initially Tony lived in the "baby cottage" with the other kids of pre-school age. I went into

Kids listen to the radio

Cottage 10, a large house that slept forty boys. There were two dormitories in the cottage, each with beds for twenty boys. There was a large living room area where we would gather and listen to the radio. We often listened to the Cleveland Indians' ball games. I remember cheering for Larry Doby, Bob Feller and other Indians players who

were the stars of the team in those days. Cleveland won the World Series in 1948 when I was eight years old.

Adventure stories were also a staple of our radio entertainment. Sister Mary Ellen was the head of our cottage and a mother to us forty kids. She had some help from one of the

Children in church on Sunday

other nuns, Sr. Mary Bernard. When television arrived, it was a very big deal, and not being allowed to watch it was a true hardship! I remember being punished in that way on occasion when I had been naughty. Sister Marie Ellen would make me sit on the steps, away from the TV, but there was a large mirror in the foyer that enabled me to see the screen anyway. I always wondered if Sister knew that.

As in most schools and institutions at the time, corporal punishment was used liberally. I remember being spanked a lot, especially when someone would beat up my brother because I would go and 'take care' of any boy who dared to pick on Tony.

I was also used to being out at night, thanks to my father's terrible example, so some nights I'd sneak out to visit a private archery range in the nearby woods, where the archers would pay us to find their lost arrows. Many nights I would wander back to the orphanage late and be punished with a good spanking. My other main punishment was scrubbing the entire basement floor on my hands and knees with kind and gentle Sister Mary Ellen standing over me with the paddle. I managed to survive the spankings, but I would never let Sister see me cry; instead, I would go somewhere private and cry alone. Tony remembers times when all the boys would be lined up together, waiting their turn to lean over the deep sink and get walloped with a fox-tail dust brush—the wooden side. This "mass walloping" only ever happened when all the boys were out of control; in which case, Sister Mary Ellen would punish us all. The guilty and the innocent.

We all attended church frequently, of course, and the feelings I would experience are still with me. The church was beautiful, and to me, as a little boy, it smelled as I thought heaven would smell.

I had a good voice, so I sang in the choir. On special occasions, like Christmas, a musician from the Cleveland Orchestra would perform with us. I loved it; the music sounded so holy when we sang. The incense smell would linger in the air throughout the mass, and, in those days, the mass was spoken in Latin. The choir received numerous requests to perform in the community, including on local radio and television broadcasts. We were also invited to perform with the St. John's Cathedral men's choir for a radio broadcast of *The Catholic Hour*, hosted by Bishop Fulton J. Sheen, which was an amazing honor for all of us.

The Christmas season was a big event at Parmadale. Each year a real sleigh pulled by horses would come to the orphanage loaded with gifts.

My brother Tony is the boy on the bottom left with the drum. Each child got to pick a gift from a list before Christmas, and that, plus a bag of candy and a piece of fruit, was our Christmas gift. We were all grateful for what we had, and I have nothing but good memories of

Christmas party in the baby cottage

Christmases at Parmadale. Tony always thought that he started to learn to play the drums while at Parmadale. When we found this picture, he realized where that memory originated. He was never in the band.

Sundays were visitors' days, and my two grandmothers would occasionally show up on alternate Sundays. We were all shiny and eager on visitors' day. Even if you did not get visitors, you would benefit because the kids that did get visitors would share the loot they got from their relatives.

Documents say that my father would visit occasionally, but I do not recall that ever happening. I do have the Catholic prayer book that he gave me though. It is the only physical item I have from my father. Our grandmothers would bring us treats sometimes on visiting day, and, of course, we would always share our goodies with the more unfortunate kids who had no one to visit them.

Parmadale had a large playground area to play in, along with

Kids on visitor's day

a football field and swimming pool. We would play marbles, roller skate and play baseball with the other kids. On April 28, 1949, there was a total lunar eclipse in the middle of a bright sunny day. I thought it was the end of the world, as I do not recall being told about the event. Everyone was scared to death.

A DAY AT PARMADALE

A typical day at Parmadale is best described by the daily schedules shown here, copied from a Parmadale history document from 1932. The routine was still in place when Tony and I moved in in 1948.

After my brother moved from the baby cottage into Cottage 10, where I stayed, I would make my bed in the morning, then go help him make his. We were early risers at Parmadale, as you can see in the schedules. This is probably why my brother and I are still early risers to this day!

Each day after play time, we would all sit on a bench and take our socks off, then turn them inside out and wear them again the next day. I don't recall having to change underwear that way, thankfully!

Evening time was shower time. The shower room held about twenty kids. We would wear shorts called shower tights, which I thought you could see through. I remember goofing off in the shower, and Sister Mary Ellen would lift the hem of her habit, step across the wet floor, and whack me with her paddle. Once I ran right out of the shower with Sister Mary Ellen in hot pursuit. She chased me around the row of sinks, through the dormitory and only God

DAILY PROGRAM
SCHOOL YEAR
1932

6:15	Rise - Monday, thru Friday
7:30	Rise - Saturday
6:45	Holy Mass - Monday thru Fri. & Sat., at 7:30 (not compulsory)
7:15	Breakfast
8:00	To Cottage
8:30	School
10:15	Recess
10:30	School
11:30	Dinner
12:00-12:45	Band Practice - 135 Boys
12:00-12:45	Recreation on School Playground for Boys Not In The Bands
12:45-1:00	Prepare for School
1:00-3:00	School
3:00-3:30	Band Practice
3:00-3:30	Choir Practice - Beginner's Choir
3:30-4:00	Choir Practice - Regular Choir
3:00-5:00	Recreation on the Playground or in the Gymnasium
5:00-5:30	Prepare for Supper
5:30-6:30	Supper
6:30-7:30	Study Hour In School - Mon, thru Thurs.
6:30-7:30	Recreation in Cottage or Gymnasium Fri.
7:30-9:00	Recreation in Cottages
9:00-9:30	Showers and Retire

SATURDAY PROGRAM

7:30 - - - - - - - - - Rise

8:00 - - - - - - - - - Breakfast

8:30 - - - - - - - - - First, Second, Third Grade Boys to Playground or Gymnasium.
Boys above third grade return to cottages
for work

10:30 - - - - - - - - - Smaller boys from gymnasium to Playground
or cottages

11:15 - - - - - - - - - Prepare for dinner

11:30 - - - - - - - - - Dinner

12:00 - 1:00 - - - - - Band Practice

12:30 - 2:30 - - - -.- Recreation on playground or in gymnasium

2:30 - 5:00 - - - - - Basketball practice with coach - varsity
squad - Winter
Football or baseball - Spring
Foorball or baseball - Autumn

2:30 - 5:00 - - - - - Smaller boys on playground, gymnasium, or
in cottages

5:30 - - - - - - - - - Supper

6:30 - 7:30 - - - - - Choir Practice for Sunday

6:30 - 8:00 - - - - - Recreation in cottages

8:00 - 9:00 - - - - - Showers and retire

knows where else. By now my shower tights had fallen off, and I was running around naked with the other kids laughing all around me. I think Sister Mary Ellen was also laughing. Of course, I received a spanking for those maneuvers when I was finally cornered—I think Sister may have even called for reinforcements to apprehend me. I still laugh when I think of this, and I suspect she probably does too.

Sister had a room at the end of the dorm with a window that opened into our room so that she could open it and look in on us. Prior to getting into bed, we would all kneel and recite our evening prayers. Usually it was uneventful, but one night one of the boys was late for evening prayers, and his entrance in the dormitory was something I will never forget. There were twenty of us kneeling and praying, and suddenly this boy came tearing in and began jumping from bed to bed, farting loudly each time he landed. Well, needless to say, that was the end of prayers! We were all laughing so hard we could not hear Sister Mary Ellen yelling at him. Boy, did he get a spanking—but probably not too hard, as Sister was probably laughing too.

The dormitory picture above shows the sisters' room and the window where she would poke her head out to scold us when we were misbehaving after lights out.

We kept the large cottage in spotless condition, dusting and polishing floors

Kids cleaning shoes

on our hands and knees. I know I got the basement clean, as I would be the one punished for something, and I would always end up on my knees scrubbing the floor. The younger boys would have their dormitory cleaned, and, if one of the boys wet his bed, he would be thrown down the dirty clothes chute. I used to help my younger brother make his

Dormitory with the Sister's room

bed in the morning. Fortunately, he was not a bed wetter!

Before television we would all sit around the radio in the evening listening to the kids' shows. When television finally arrived, we would all hurry after supper to run back to the cottage in time for *Hopalong Cassidy*.

Dinner was something else! I recall having to fight older kids as they would grab your bread and dessert or whatever else they could grab. One had to fight or threaten to call Sister Mary Ellen before they ate your food.

We prayed before we ate, we prayed at bedtime, and it seemed to me we prayed before just about everything. I said enough prayers and attended church so often that I thought it was enough for my entire lifetime.

On laundry day we would stand in line to receive our clean clothes. I always tried to get in front of the line, as there was always pushing and shoving to receive the best clothes. No one wanted to get short pants or knickers. Usually it worked out that the older/bigger kids got first choice.

MEMORIES FROM PARMADALE

There were many military airfields in Ohio, and I loved to watch the airplanes flying over in formation. I had books about the different types of military planes and could identify most of them as I sat under a tree watching the sky for planes. I really wanted to become a fighter pilot some day, and, much later in life, I did in fact became a commercial pilot and flight instructor.

One of my best memories was the day we were told we could choose an instrument to play. I had always wanted to play a trumpet, just like our guest musician from the Cleveland Orchestra. But when it was my turn to choose an instrument, they had run out of trumpets, so I got a clarinet instead. Luckily, I learned to love it, and I practiced many hours a day.

Outdoor band practice

As an adult, I did become an accomplished clarinet player; I also learned to play the saxophone. The great baseball player Ted Williams had an event at the Cleveland Stadium, and the Parmadale Band was selected to play for it. Our band was also featured in Cleveland's parades; even though our school only went to the eighth grade, we were very accomplished and sought-after musicians. I liked marching when Parmadale was the lead band in a parade and would puff out my chest and play like my life depended on it.

During the year, some Cleveland civic groups would take some of us to go fishing or to the ball games. We also went to Euclid Beach once a year to enjoy the rides and the food. We were treated by different charitable groups who would sponsor our day at the park. The kids were ecstatic when these opportunities came along!

There were wonderful hills nearby for sled riding in the wintertime. They were located near the cottages. Each cottage had a couple of sleds for any kid who wanted to ride the snow. We would check in with the nun assigned to watch the activity that day. S'ter (short pronunciation of "Sister") was wrapped in a heavy shawl and tasked with keeping an eye out for trouble. There were many hills, and they all had names like "Devil Hill," "Snake Hill," "Dead Man's Dive" and "Popeye's Muscle." Some of the younger nuns would take a turn on the sled, but they were not peppered with snowballs at the bottom of the hill by the boys waiting their turn like the rest of us were.

There were apple trees on the property where we got to go pick some, and, of course, there was usually an "apple fight".

I remember protecting my brother from the others, especially the bullies. I got to be tough when I had to defend my little brother. I recall the nuns using a hand brush to strike us on our hands when we misbehaved. I would dance around in circles when receiving this punishment, but I would not let them see me cry. Sometimes, they would pull down our pants to strike us on our bare bottoms. I put magazines or papers in my pants but would always get caught. That is why they would pull the pants down.

Once I ran away, and the nuns chased me up a hillside on State Road quite far from Parmadale. I did not think they could run so fast in their habits, but they caught me and returned me to the orphanage. I was punished, and I knew I deserved it.

FINAL THOUGHTS ON PARMADALE

Even though I mostly enjoyed my time at Parmadale, I always had many questions in the back of my mind; for instance, where were my sisters? And why couldn't our relatives keep us all together? As a child, I thought this was terribly unfair of them, but as an adult I realize that times were probably too hard during those years for a family to take on four additional mouths to feed. My mother's sisters were very young when my mother died, so they were not capable of taking us in, and our two grandmothers were considered too old to look after Tony and me. I also wondered where my father was; although, by this time I barely remembered him.

When I was older, I began to appreciate the difficult job the nuns had had to do. They could not give each child the individual love that only a mother and father could give, as each sister had forty or so young kids to take care of. They could not reach out to us as individuals, like a mother and a father might. But despite these limitations, they did a wonderful job. They made us strong and self-reliant, skills they knew we would need in life, even more so than kids who had grown up in intact families. I know now that these devoted sisters are the ones who taught me basic survival.

On September 24, 1950, Parmadale began its Silver Jubilee celebration. On hand to greet visitors were eight 25-year veterans of service to the kids. Included in this group was Sister Mary Ellen and Mr. Jack Hearns, to whom I owe so much. Many alumni went on to have successful careers.

Once, in the early sixties, I took my young wife to Parmadale; in those years, it was still an orphanage. It did not look as big as I remembered. We knocked at the door to Cottage 10, and when the door opened, there stood Sister Mary Ellen. She remembered me and said something like, "How many times did I spank you?" My wife and I stayed with her for a while. It was gratifying to visit with her, and I will never forget her. She has since passed away, but I know where she is, as Sister Mary Ellen was a saint. I am grateful to her and have the utmost respect for her on the job she did raising us for four and a half years.

Parmadale orphanage is no more, as foster care and adoptions have taken their place as preferred solutions to kids in need of homes. Parmadale had its share of scandals and troubles over the years, but I never witnessed any of that other than the corporal punishment that today would not be tolerated.

If you search for Parmadale on the internet, you will find stories of abuse by the sisters told by many people who were there as kids. You will also find people with positive memories of their time at Parmadale. The corporal punishment we received would certainly be described as abuse today, but in those days, corporal punishment was not uncommon.

I am sure that there are kids who were abused in other ways over the years, and that is totally evil. It is terrible that all the good that was done at Parmadale is sullied by the evil deeds of a few.

Aerial view of Parmadale as it was when it was an orphanage. You can see the sledding hills on the top far right. The row of cottages on the left were the girls' and preschoolers' cottages. On the right is the row of boys' cottages. The school building is in the center, and the dining hall is in the background.

I know that is not true today. No matter what happened at Parmadale, I will always have fond memories of my time there. I always said when my two children were growing up, that if I or my wife should die for some reason, that I would want my children to go to an orphanage like Parmadale, rather than growing up in an unhappy home.

If you had to live in an orphanage, Parmadale was as good as it got.

Today, I don't believe the spankings affected me at all in my later life. As I stated, I have nothing but fond memories of Parmadale. I believe the upbringing I had at Parmadale made me the person I am today. I learned to survive and achieve anything I wanted in life. The achievements and challenges in life I faced stem from my early childhood at Parmadale.

Sister Mary Ellen was my mother and the mother to forty other children. I'm sure she has been rewarded with her place in heaven.

ADIOS PARMADALE

From the Cleveland Plain Dealer September 22, 2018, Grant Segall

Parma-One of many graffiti on the walls at Parmadale says "Witness the End".

The end began Friday morning as an excavator tore into the brick walls, concrete floors, and slate roofs of one of the 1925 Tudor-style dormitories (modestly called cottages) at this widely beloved, sometimes hated Catholic orphanage turned treatment center and future parkland.

Karl, front left, with brother Tony, front right and Cousin Jack (visiting) standing in front of cottage ten circa, 1948.

Former residents say it's inevitable but sad to see their old home become part of the adjacent West Creek Reservation.

"There are a lot of emotions there," said John Abraham, a resident, house father and activities director for decades.

Like many Catholic institutions and former orphanages, the 93-year-old Parmadale became controversial in later years. A few workers were convicted of sexual offenses against residents. Three were fired but acquitted in a 17-year-old's death under restraint.

But alumni of the orphanage say they saw no abuse. Instead they remember strict but loving nuns, overseeing a cottage of 40 children.

The nuns woke the youngsters at 6:15 AM. They shut the lights off at 9:30 pm. They passed out toothbrushes for scrubbing each cottage. No wonder the place was dubbed "Parmajail."

But alumni also remember finding lucky coins hidden in pancakes, splashing in an outdoor pool, tossing horseshoes, and picking Christmas gifts from Sears. Barbequing hot dogs on bedsprings, wolfing down fried chicken and mashed potatoes on Sundays, catching turkeys for Thanksgiving feasts, and chopping down trees in 52 acres of woods for forts and tepees are even more memories from the orphanage.

"Can you imagine giving kids axes today?" Marvels Marylyn Osborne, who graduated in 1967.

Mike Funtash, there during the 1950s. says, "Every kid there wanted to go home, of course. But it was really nice. You had good food, doctors, nurses, all kinds of activities."

Residents attended a school on the Parmadale campus through to the eighth grade. They also won championships in local sports leagues, sang at downtown hotels and paraded with President Harry Truman and John Phillip Sousa. They won that maestro's coveted Sousa Cup as the nation's best band in its age group.

Laura Martz, a resident on and off from the late 1960s into the early 1980s, says of Parmadale, "I loved it. It was a place of refuge. We were all people with like issues. We could all come together as a family."

From the beginning, few residents were true orphans. Most came because of illness, poverty, divorce and other problems at home. Parents visited on Sundays if they could.

Says Osborne, "We never talked about why we were there. Only when we reconnected years later did we start telling our stories."

Parmadale was billed as the nation's first "cottage village" for children. It sat on more than 100 acres along State Road in Parma. On a clear day, you can see downtown from the curb.

It hosted just boys at first but then went co-ed in 1947. The nuns tried to break the ice with a dance. The boys lined up on one wall and the girls the other. No one mingled until ice cream and cake arrived.

Many alumni went on to successful careers. Dennis Kucinich spent a few months here before his years in Cleveland City Hall and Congress.

Orphanages have dwindled in recent decades in favor of foster care and adoption. In the 1980s, Parmadale started focusing more on youths *with special needs. Parts of the campus were gradually turned over to other Catholic agencies.*

In 2013, after the resident's death under restraint, Ohio put Parmadale on probation. Soon the site closed its residential programs in favor of daytime treatment. Weeds, weather and vandals went to work.

"It's like a hurricane went through," says Eric Tolerup, Parma's community development director. "It's a shame. These buildings were once quite beautiful."

Adios to a former orphanage

Parmadale being torn down
Grant Segall, Cleveland Plain Dealer 9/22/2018

CHAPTER TWO

FOSTER HOMES

IN SEPTEMBER OF 1952, MY aunt and uncle Minello took me from the orphanage to live with them in Painesville, Ohio. My aunt Evelyn, my mother's older sister, was married to John Minello. Evelyn was a homemaker and an excellent Italian cook. My uncle Johnny, a self-employed plumber, was a taciturn man who worked hard and made a good living. They had two kids at the time, Jack, who was a few years older than me, and Lyn, who was younger than me by a few years. They eventually had another son, Vincent. I turned twelve the month after I moved in with the Minello family. Although the Minellos were sponsors at my baptism, I have few memories of them prior to moving into their home. I never did learn why they decided to take me then, after years in the orphanage, rather than immediately after my mother's death.

Their home was in Painesville Township, which was a beautiful place to live. It was country living, with many nurseries with fields of roses as far as one's eyes could see. We lived next to the Lake County Fairgrounds. I attended St. Mary's Catholic school in Painesville for the seventh and eighth grades. After St. Mary's, I attended high school at Riverside High.

My brother also left Parmadale Orphanage and was sent to live with another of our mother's sisters, Claire. Claire was very young and recently married to Nick Cunovic. They lived in Cleveland, where they enrolled Tony in the local elementary school. Tony lived with the Cunovics for three months when our social worker, Miss Green, showed up at his school and took him out of class. Miss Green had Tony's bag packed and drove him to the foster home of Ted and Elizabeth DeWitte in Middleburgh Hts. Ohio, a suburb of Cleveland. Tony never heard from our Aunt Claire again. We always wondered what prompted this rapid eviction from his new home. Tony has always assumed that he was just too much for the young couple.

I look back on the early days when I first came to Painesville to live with my aunt and uncle and the memories I have of life with them. We would gather around the television on Saturday nights and watch the Saturday night fights and eat popcorn. We also watched the honeymooners, Jackie Gleason and Art Carney. We all laughed and enjoyed the shows a lot. We always had good Italian food, especially on Sundays. My aunt would always make my lunch when I was working in the local nurseries like Bosley's, Martin's, Wayside and others.

I mentioned that my aunt and uncle also had a daughter when I lived with them, and later they had a baby boy. I don't remember very much about Lynn but remember that Jack teased her a lot and would cause trouble between them and their mom and dad. Jack would usually get yelled at for his antics.

I liked to ride my bike around with other kids in the neighborhood. We would ride to the construction site where the shopping center was being built, which was around 1954. There was a swimming hole that we used to go to in summertime. It was in Painesville Township where the local sand and gravel business was located. A lot of us would jump off the equipment, which was close enough for us to jump into the water. We did not wear swimming trunks at time because we would get out of the water and play in the real soft mud adjacent to the pond. The boys and I would lie in the hot sun and let the mud cake dry onto our skin and climb onto the crane and jump into the water. We would spend hours at the pond, which, if I remember right, was spring fed. One day quite a few of us were on top of the crane, naked and ready to jump into the water when someone yelled,

"Here comes some girls on their bikes!" I looked over to see where the girls were, and the other boys were already jumping off the crane into the water. I also jumped off into the pond.

My uncle had grapevines in the garden area, and my aunt would have Jack and I pick the ripening grapes off the vine. She would make the best tasting grape jam I had ever tasted; I would have homemade Italian bread with peanut butter and jelly. My other favorite was the eggplant sandwiches.

COUSIN JACK

My cousin Jack and I became great friends and spent a lot of time together, even though he was older than me. Jack really liked to work on cars and to hunt, shoot, and fish. We hunted rabbits and squirrels during the season, which we would clean for my aunt to use in the spaghetti sauce. Spaghetti con scoiattolo! I can still smell the Italian foods that she prepared; I especially loved the eggplant sandwiches.

Jack and I spent a great deal of time in the woods in and around Lake County. I still have a picture of him and me together. Jack always reminded me of Hank Williams, the popular country singing star. Jack and I slept in the same bed upstairs in the new house my uncle built in 1954. Jack had a target

Jack on the (left) with Karl

on the wall in our bedroom for throwing knives. When Jack came to bed, he often stunk like grease and oil, as he enjoyed working on cars whenever he could.

Jack would frequently sneak out the bedroom window at night and go to the store nearby to buy beer and cigarettes. Our friend's dad owned the store, so that's how Jack was able to get the beer. I would haul the beer and cigarettes up from the window with a fishing pole. We would get silly and loud in the wee hours of the morning, causing my uncle to yell swear words at us in Italian from downstairs.

The first time I smoked a cigarette, a Lucky Strike, I was in the upstairs bathroom sitting on the pot. If you were around in those days, you know that smoking was considered very cool and acceptable. There was a popular commercial "LSMFT," meaning Luck Strike Means Fine Tobacco. I thought I was cool, but it did not taste very good and I coughed the whole time.

Jack had a set of drums, and we would play music together in the downstairs family room. There was a bar in there as well, and we would make drinks using his dad's booze, then fill the rest of the bottle back up with water to fool my uncle. My uncle, nobody's fool, caught on quickly, and we caught hell for that.

Once I started at Riverside High School, I was supposed to attend catechism classes on the nights that my uncle would bowl. I would always skip the class and hang out in downtown Painesville.

I started a paper route in the neighborhood to earn my own spending money, which I mostly saved to buy a new clarinet. The first clarinet I purchased was a brand-new wooden Noblet, a French brand. It was costly at the time, but it had a wonderful sound. I used to practice on it many hours a day.

After my daily paper route was completed, I would fill the canvas bags up from the vegetable gardens that I would pass on my way home. I arrived home with the bags full of fresh fruits and vegetables. All my customers on my new route knew me well and would comment that they knew I was coming by my whistling. They ignored my vegetable "shopping" from their gardens.

I was a happy kid when I was twelve but could never get close to my aunt and uncle. I could never call anyone Mom or Dad. When I was thirteen, I bought my uncle a red maple tree for Father's Day; we planted it at the side of his new house. Forty-six years later, when I returned to Ohio from Alaska, the tree had grown into a full-size beautiful red maple. The site where the house had stood was now a used-car lot, but that tree always reminded me of that wonderful day when my uncle and I had planted it. Then, one year, the management of the car lot had the tree cut down to make room for eight more cars. The day I drove by and saw it missing, I could not stop myself from crying. It was a crushing loss of something that had been indescribably precious to me. I am still devastated about that tree being cut down.

While attending St. Mary's elementary school, I received an invitation to a Halloween party out in the country. It was to be a square dance, but alas, I did not know how to square dance. The invitation requested that I bring a bag of marshmallows to roast around the campfire. Well, my uncle dropped me off at the location of the party—just me and my bag of marshmallows—and then drove off again before I discovered that there was no party! One of my classmates had pulled a great joke on me, and even though I was a bit miffed, I had to laugh. They had gotten me fair and square. I hitchhiked home and told my aunt and uncle, who laughed until they cried. It was a great joke, and I never did find out who sent me that invitation.

During the summers, I worked at the nurseries for $0.35 an hour. I would go from one nursery to another, wherever there was work. I worked with many Mexican men who would teach us kids to swear in Spanish. I still remember some of those naughty words today.

While I was in the seventh and eighth grades, I played on the football team. I would ride my bike to the practice field, wearing my uniform. I had a friend who lived next door to the now-famous NFL coach of the Miami Dolphins, Don Shula in Grand River, Ohio.

A TYPICAL PRETEEN

One day, after school hours were over, my friend and I were in the auditorium for some reason; perhaps we needed to practice for a school play or something. A female classmate of mine wandered into the auditorium, grabbed me by the hand and, while giggling, started to run with me holding my hand. What the heck was going on? She took me behind the stage area into a small room, pushed me onto a table and began humping me. I did not know what the hell she was doing, but she was humping me so hard, she was hurting me. My friend came looking for me. He heard a female voice and followed it, opened the door, and saved the day for me. She got off me and left the room. I was stupid about girls then but later understood what she was attempting to do. WHEW! My friend was laughing hard about the incident, and I started laughing and could not stop. I still have these laughing fits that others cannot stop from joining. I laugh so hard and long that my stomach hurts.

Another incident occurred while the student body was attending a play in the auditorium. It was a Shakespearean type play. All was quiet in the auditorium during this scene. It was the silliest sight I had ever seen; a young skinny boy wearing tight leotards prancing across the stage. I just lost it. It was the silliest sight that I had ever seen. I started laughing and could not stop. Others in the audience began laughing at my laughing. The play was stopped, and boy was I in trouble now. I was still laughing as the principal came down the aisle to my seat, grabbed my ear, and yanked me up the aisle to the exit. The audience was still laughing loudly as I was dragged out of the auditorium. The principal took me to his office where I was still laughing behind closed doors. He cracked me a few times, but I laughed louder. I guess I finally stopped and was kicked out of school for a few days for the outburst. I really did not mean to stop the play the way I did, but to this day, I haven't seen anything so funny as when that kid in the black-tight pants pranced across the stage.

The same teacher that produced the play was the public speaking teacher, and I was in his class. One day, the class was told that we were to approach the front, pick a topic out of a hat and speak on the topic for two minutes. When my turn came, I was prepared to tackle the assignment. I picked my topic out of the hat; it was "How I made my first dollar." I looked up at the class and began "I made my first dollar..." but suddenly began laughing so hard that the teacher had his head with a beet red face from laughing at me, bent over on his desk. The whole class was laughing. My laugh is so contagious that everyone joins in, but I cannot control it. After a minute or so the red-faced teacher exclaimed, "Mr. Lewkowski, get out of my class!" Well, that ended my career in public speaking.

A LAST VISIT FROM MY FATHER

I was about thirteen years old when my father came to my uncle's house. I was told to get upstairs right away, which I did, and my uncle went outside to the cab in the driveway. My father was drunk, and my uncle would not let me see him in that condition. I know I cried when he left, but my uncle was only looking out for my welfare. I was saddened because that was the last chance I would have to see my father alive. I never did see him again. He died on June 14, 1957, when I was seventeen. I still regret that day that I was unable to see him, but I do understand my uncle wanting to protect me.

My brother Tony was in a foster home at the time. He remembers getting a phone call informing him that his dad had died. Tony was fourteen and remembers that he cried for a while after the call. It was about this time that Tony started to get in trouble, leading to his discharge from the foster home.

TEEN YEARS

There were many times the atmosphere at my uncle's house was unbearable for me unless Jack and his friends were there. I knew that I could not talk to my uncle about anything, and there was silence when I was around. If they asked me questions, I would remain silent. I don't think Jack was dating very much at the time, and my aunt and uncle could not cope with me dating someone and wanting to be with Toni all the time. Looking back, I needed Toni and she needed me. At the time we met at the fair, I wanted to be with her in all of my spare time. It was 1956 when I was in the eleventh grade and life was not too pleasant for me, as I was not getting along too well with my uncle. I would stay out with my friends and not return to the house till late at night. I remember my friends would drop me off in the evening, perhaps later than I should have been. As usual, the doors would be locked, and I would climb onto the roof and pound on the window so Jack could let me in. I cannot recall the type of punishment I would receive but was aware of the silent treatment. Having been in the orphanage until I was twelve, I can only relate to a family environment from my experiences at Parmadale. Living with my aunt and uncle since 1952 was my first experience outside of the orphanage that I can remember. I did not relate very well, and I remember feeling that I did not belong. As I said earlier, my first year or two with them seemed to be as normal as I thought it could be. I never recall being struck by my aunt and uncle or abused in any way. I truly do believe they were good people who were not able to put up with my feelings, nor could I ever relate my feelings to them. I do not recall any type of personal close relationship with my aunt or uncle, nor do I recall any type of affection or feelings of being loved. They provided me with food, shelter, clothing, and the necessities of life.

I was very close to Jack and felt as if he were my brother. We got along well in every way. I obtained a report from my caseworker from the welfare department later in life, which read:

Karl is a boy that, as young child, was described as shy, quiet and not one that related easily to adults, as he seemed unable to discuss the situation in the foster home. The uncle, on the other hand, is an excitable person who seems to store his feelings until there is explosion. The maternal aunt is a quiet individual who tries to counteract her husband's excitable nature. One would question the reasoning anyone would have in talking to a person of the husband's disposition. Karl also appears to be a boy who was led and influenced into misbehavior by his peers. It was felt by the schools that Karl's difficulties were partially due to such influences, as well as the situation in his home in general.

Further on, the report describes my schoolwork:

Karl is a bright boy of probably superior intelligence. He is in the eleventh grade at Riverside High School in Painesville. It is felt his schoolwork is good enough but could do much better if he tried harder. He is quite talented in music and plays in the school band. He is also a first-string halfback and is considered a very good player considering his size. Karl also expresses an interest in going to college ...

Karl is an intelligent, attractive boy. His primary interest is football and other sports and his music. Karl's band recently joined the musician's union and plays at school dances. He has many friends in Painesville, and his interests seem typical of a boy his age. He enjoys going out with his group of friends in the evening but does not return home until after the hour requested by his aunt.

As I entered my teenage years, my relationship with my uncle started going downhill. I never felt like a son, nor could I ever talk to my aunt and uncle as if they were my parents. I was never mistreated, but at times they would lose their tempers with me as I grew older. I was becoming a teenager, and I wanted to run my own life as I saw fit. Like so many teenage boys, I needed something but did not know what it was. Maybe being an orphan brought on these feelings.

One New Year's Eve, I was in downtown Painesville with some of the guys who had some Italian homemade wine. Of course, I had to try some too, as everyone else was drinking. I became intoxicated very quickly, and the police found me banging on the bank building with my shoe. The police called my uncle to come pick me up, and he obviously wasn't too happy.

Jack and his friends would let me go with them in their old cars. We liked to drive around town; sometimes they had guns in their cars and would shoot at various targets, such as stop signs. We also loved to go to the dump and shoot rats. One Halloween there must have been twelve of us in a '47 Ford with the backseats out. We were driving around in the country and decided it would be funny to let a farmer's cows out of their pasture. One of my friends got out of the car and attempted to ride on the back of one of the cows. We drove by much later to find the police rounding the cows up. I wish that I could apologize to those police officers and that farmer today.

I remember wearing secondhand clothes and feeling that I dressed "funny." When I got to high school, one of my friends and I started going to downtown Painesville and stealing clothes. We would walk out of the store with sweaters, shirts and shoes. I would hide my new outfits in my school locker and change into them when I got to school; I wanted to dress as nice as the other kids. I also remember my friends stealing records from the record store and selling them at school. I only stole what I thought I needed to look presentable. I am not proud of the stealing, however, and would make it right today if I could.

One day I was riding around in downtown Painesville with some older boys in a '52 Plymouth. We were just riding around acting cool, as teenagers liked to do. We were driving by the courthouse when we saw a parking meter that had been knocked down. One of the older boys I was with told me to get out and retrieve the parking meter. I retrieved it and jumped in the backseat of the car thinking, foolishly, that we were going to turn it in. Instead, one of the boys in the front seat gave me a hammer and told me to start breaking it open. I obeyed and started breaking the meter; coins were flying all over the backseat. While driving toward Fairport, Ohio, we turned onto the road to Grand River, stopping at the railroad tracks. A police car drove up behind us with flashing lights and its siren going. My friends and I in the backseat began frantically picking up coins, placing them in our gloves and hiding them in the back of the armrest. When the police car was beside us, I opened the right-side door and tossed out the remaining parts of the parking meter. The police took us back to the station for questioning. Apparently, someone had seen us take the meter and called the cops.

The policeman went into a room, took off his gun belt and hung it up on the clothes rack. I was so scared thinking of what my uncle would do when he found out that I jokingly went for the gun.

One of the older guys said, "What the hell are you doing?" and pushed me away from the gun. It was such a dumb thing to do, but I was really scared. When the cops were done questioning us, we were released. I don't recall why we were let go, but I suppose the police ultimately believed that we'd found the meter already knocked over.

Jack, his friends, and I liked to camp out at Indian Point Park in the summertime. The park was just southeast of Painesville. We drank beer, hiked a lot and sat by the campfire just goofing off. Jack's friends were three or four years older than me, but I hung out with them quite a bit. They had fast cars like Jack and liked to hunt, shoot, drink beer and raise a little hell. We all seemed to get along great. I always had fun when I was with Jack. He was like an older brother to me during the time I spent at my aunt and uncle's home.

My life seemed idyllic at the time, but I was uneasily aware of the way I felt inside. I was tired of being told how to live my life by everyone, especially by the welfare department and my aunt and uncle. I don't feel like they were bad people; I was never abused, nor do I recall being hit or spanked by them. I just wanted to be on my own and make my own decisions and live the life I wanted to live—be the person I wanted to be. I wanted my father to be around. I missed my brother, Tony, and worried about how he was doing. I thought of my two little sisters and wondered where they were, how they were growing up. Most of all, I wanted to be in control of my life. Obviously, I was *not* in control and never had been, and I was beginning to resent that.

I do not remember exactly when it started, but it may have been in the ninth grade or so: I started noticing girls—not that I knew anything about them. I also started wanting to dress in nicer clothes, partly to impress girls and partly just to blend in with my classmates. Sometimes this went fine, and other times it really did not. For example, once I was invited to a Halloween party (a real one this time!), and I stole a black pair of pegged pants and an orange shirt, thinking it would fit the Halloween color theme. I knew stealing clothes or anything else was not the right thing to do, but I was uncomfortable around other kids and wanted to be more like them. I thought I looked rather good in this outfit, but I still didn't feel as if I was one of them.

I think the event that clinched it for me was the time the family went to dinner at an immensely popular restaurant near my aunt and uncle's home. I will never forget the way I was dressed that evening: checkered pants and a Hawaiian printed shirt that did not match at all. I was embarrassed to death and vowed never to look like that again. My aunt and uncle were good people, and I reasoned that perhaps they could not afford to buy me clothes. So, being a resourceful kid, I took matters into my own hands.

As I said, however, things had begun to go downhill for me in terms of my relationship with my aunt and uncle; I know I am partly to blame for this. It was not that I hated them; I just wanted to control my own life. Was it because of the way I was raised in the orphanage, to be independent and self-reliant? I do not know. Did I feel like, as the oldest brother, I was responsible for my brother and sisters? I didn't even know where my sisters were. I thought of them and my brother all the time, and my sadness and guilt and frustration and anger churned around inside me.

I began to stay out late with some of my friends who had cars, and that swiftly turned into not coming home at all. I slept in used-car lots where I would find open vehicles and go from there to school when I woke up in the morning. At times, I would sleep under the bridge down by the river near the high school, using a pile of leaves for comfort. I was not a bad kid, but I was a troubled boy who was rebellious and confused. I am sure that a child psychologist could have helped me overcome my angst, but those were few and far between where we lived.

My friend Kenny would drop me off at my uncle's house late at night and leave. My uncle would lock the doors, and I could not get in. I would climb up on the roof to knock on the window to have my cousin Jack let me in. If Jack was not home, I would sleep out at used-car lots, as most of the car doors were open.

I would occasionally sleep down by the river by the high school and sometimes near Route 20 in a pile of leaves. I was scared to go home at night and did not want to endure the wrath of my aunt and uncle. I would awake in the morning and walk to school or hitch a ride whenever I could. When I was by the river under the bridge, I would walk to school. At times my friends would be out looking for me at night to find me, but I don't remember them ever being successful. I had become fairly good at keeping myself hidden.

In later life, however, I have learned that the adults around me, particularly my teachers, were keenly aware of what was happening and kept an eye out for me. Thirty years later, when I returned to Lake County from Alaska, I was at a local restaurant when I saw one of my high school teachers who was having his retirement party at the restaurant. He noticed me right away. He came over, shook my hand, and said, "Karl, I will never forget you." I asked him why, and he stated, "One day you came to school quite dirty and muddy, and I asked you where you had been all night. You nonchalantly answered that you had slept down by the river under the bridge."

He had never forgotten that, and I was astonished that he had remembered me. I believe that most of the teachers I had were very understanding of the circumstances of my life. I liked most of them, especially my band teacher, Mr. Richard Denner. I will always remember him as being an important part of my life.

Sometimes, I think I can play the role of a psychiatrist and analyze my behavioral problems. During the early days of my life, neither I nor my brother received the love and tenderness that a normal child would have with a real mother and father. Sister Mary Ellen was my mother figure, along with thirty-nine other kids she cared for. I know she loved all of us and completed her motherly role the best she could. She was a wonderful nun, along with all the staff at the orphanage. There is no doubt in my mind that Sister Mary Ellen was welcomed in heaven by a host of angels and almighty God. May she rest in peace. I knew I deserved all the spankings and honestly believe she was a factor in making me the person I turned out to be.

Mr. and Mrs. Johnson were also a major factor in my development and, after them, there would be several more persons who greatly affected my life. When I left the orphanage, it seemed that I always wanted to be the center of attention—showing off, if you will. I loved being the center of attention on the stage while playing in our band. I was always goofing off and making jokes. I guess I needed the attention. I sure laughed a lot and enjoyed making others laugh. I turned out to be a real chauvinist pig while growing up, and luckily, I never had to take orders from a female during my career. Did Sister Mary Ellen have anything to do with that?

THE START OF A LIFELONG LOVE OF MUSIC

I practiced my clarinet, hung out with friends, and began noticing girls who I enjoyed being with. I know on several occasions an older girl with a car used to pick me up at my uncle's house. My aunt and uncle were puzzled by this and thought it was quite odd. I was also involved with a group of guys from school who were also in the school band. We started our own band and practiced many nights together at my friend's house, which was just up the street.

When I entered the ninth grade, I began to play the clarinet in the high school band and was soon promoted to first chair clarinet. I loved playing music, and I would practice for hours every day. I regularly skipped study halls and went up to the band room with my clarinet. In school years 1955 and '56, I received a superior rating on the clarinet at a local contest. My band teacher, Mr. Denner, who I was very close to, was proud of this accomplishment. I was the only one to receive a superior rating, and I still have the award certificate. I played a difficult classical piece for the contest and spent many hours practicing for the event.

One day, while practicing in the band room, a new set of timpani drums was delivered. One of the female clarinet players was with me at the time. I sometimes played the snare drums in the marching band when another drummer was needed. I opened all the windows and began playing those timpani drums as if I were a Zulu warrior in Africa. I was chanting wildly and yelling while beating on the drums such that I did not hear the principal or the band teacher pounding on the band room doors. When I finally stopped playing the drums, I could hear laughter coming from the entire school. The sound of me yelling and beating on the drums was heard by most of the students and teachers in the entire school. I finally opened the band room doors to let the teachers into the room. I do not really recall getting kicked out of school or punished for that activity.

We were trying to come up with a name for our newly formed band. We talked to the principal and asked him for a suggestion. He said, "Why not Joe Commode and the Four Flushers?" as we had five band members. He made us all laugh, and we laughed for several minutes. I told him we would play our latest hit, "I don't give a shit for you." We all had a hilarious laugh for that comment. Like they say, those were the days. We later named our group "The Aristocrats," which was a name we had on our musician's union cards that we carried. We had a trumpet player, trombone player, pianist, a drummer and me on the clarinet and saxophone.

We began to get high school gigs playing at school dances and other venues in the community. A new group called Bill Haley and the Comets came to town, and our band got to play before the Comets came on. We were really into their type of rock 'n' roll. I desperately needed a new reed for my sax, and their sax player gave me one!

There was another group in town that played mostly polkas, and they asked me to play the drums for them at a local dance. I never had so much fun and really enjoyed the evening. I recall when it was time for us to quit, the crowd started yelling, "Let the drummer stay!" The leader in the band was not happy, and I wasn't asked to play with them again.

Another time a rock 'n' roll band was in Painesville, several of my friends were with me at the concert. One of the musicians came to the microphone and asked if there was a drummer in the audience. Their drummer could not perform, as he was sick. My friends were pushing for me to raise my hand and offer to play. I did not raise my hand. and another boy raised his hand and went to play on stage. I remember he lasted one song. There was another call for a drummer, so I did raise my hand this time and played until the concert was over.

To my knowledge, we never recorded the times we played in public. I have lost contact with the boys but would have liked to ask any of them if they had recordings of the time we were together. If I had one real skill as a kid, it was music.

One evening we played at a Township park dance on New Year's Eve. Our contract stated that we would play to one am. The audience was chanting for us to stay longer. We agreed but advised them we would need to pass the hat around for us to stay. We collected more money in the hat than we earned for the entire gig. Most of them were effected by the drinks and having a good time but were very generous.

GIRLS

One of my best friends was Dick Profeta. His dad had a small convenience store near my uncle's house on Route 20. We would ride our bikes around the surrounding neighborhoods and just hang out together. He was about a year older than me and hung around with my other soon-to-be friend, Kenny Schraufl, who was also about a year older than me. The three of us hung out together most of the time after school and weekends. Soon there were four of us with Tommy Johnson joining us. We were all on the football team in high school with Kenny at fullback, Tommy at tackle, Dick at end, and I was right halfback.

It was time for Dick and Kenny to get their driver's licenses and their own vehicles. I remember Dick's car was a '55 Chevrolet, black and white, with a sun visor and Continental kit on the back. We would cruise the local restaurants, such as Manners, which had carhops. At the time, Kenny had a '51 Ford, which was also a very sharp car.

One night we dressed up to look a little older, as we were going to the Roxy Burlesque Show in downtown Cleveland. We were not old enough to get in, but we managed to do so, as we may have looked old enough with our hats on, or our money was good. During the show, we kept our hats on until an usher told us to remove them or leave. We took the hats off.

We would regularly drive to Geneva-on-the-Lake and cruise the streets looking for girls. One evening I was not with the guys when they ran into three girls who they befriended. Dick called me a week or so later and said that we had four girls lined up to be dates and that mine was sharp. Dick had arranged to take the girls to Euclid Beach. Dick, Kenny, Tommy and I often went to Euclid Beach, which was a great place full of rides, food, and fun.

We drove north to Geneva-on-the-Lake to pick up the girls. Dick, Tommy's, and Kenny's girls were nice looking. In fact, I thought the one that Kenny had would be my date. I was wrong. The girl for me was about five inches taller than me and quite skinny. Boy was I set up. We drove to Euclid Beach, with Kenny, Dick and Tommy trying hard to hold back their laughter. The girl I was with kept on asking me to play the clarinet for her as she also played. I was glad I did not have the instrument with me, but she wanted to set up another time to hear me play. What an embarrassing night I had, and I really felt sorry for the girl. Euclid Beach had a ride called Laugh In The Dark. Most of the time it would be a good place for young lovers to enjoy some privacy. I ended up going on the ride but was not in love and did not sit close to the girl. I was trying to be as polite as possible while the other guys were obviously enjoying my predicament. I was as nice as I could be to her, as I felt sorry for her. It all ended up well, but I was glad when the evening was over. On the way home, after taking the girls home, I thought the guys were going to pass out from laughing.

Another night Dick called and said that he had found a date for me and that Dick, Kenny, Tommy and I were going to a lake down in southern Ohio to take the girls for a picnic and a boat ride. Dick drove and picked up his girl, Kenny and Tommy's girls were good-looking, then we drove to pick up my date. I had a bad feeling something was wrong when I saw this lady on the front porch who I thought was my date's mother. Was I ever wrong, as the girl walked off the porch carrying a large cake? I would estimated her weight to be at least 180 pounds while she was walking to the car. Dick's face was beet red, trying not to laugh. This was my date. I was so embarrassed for her as Dick continued to laugh, pretending he was laughing at something else, and I really tried to be nice to her all afternoon.

We even took a boat ride together, just her and me. Dick was in his boat with his head so red trying so hard to hold his laughter inside. I was, again, the target of a practical joke, which was quite mean. I tried so hard to be nice to her that afternoon without hurting her feelings.

Little did I know that life would soon present me with someone with whom I was destined to spend a lifetime.

CHAPTER THREE

THE LOVE OF MY LIFE

IN AUGUST 1956, MY FRIEND Kenny and I went to the County Fairgrounds for the annual County Fair. That day turned out to be the most important day of my life. Kenny and I were walking through the fair when we saw two young girls walking in front of us. I made some stupid teenage comment to Kenny about one of the girls. Kenny and I approached them and began talking with them. One girl's name was Toni. I later discovered that her full name was Margaret Louise Brown. It was love at first sight for me. Toni was petite, pretty, and had a smile that would melt ice cream. I knew that I had to meet her again and soon. Shortly after my first encounter with Toni, I was with another girl from Mentor who knew Toni well. I used this friendship to see Toni again at her home. I was smitten and totally unaware of how my life was about to change.

After meeting Toni again, I could not live without seeing her daily. She was the only person I wanted to be with and talk to. My friend Kenny would drive me to see Toni, and soon he became friends with Toni's sister Bonnie. We four would go out on dates together and drive around in Kenny's 1951 Ford. Toni had recently lost her father and missed him very much. Mr. Brown had died from tuberculosis and had been in the sanitarium for about three years. Being only sixteen years old and loving her father with all her heart and soul, his death was devastating to her. Toni would tell me how she would sit on his lap, especially when she had bad headaches. He would comfort and console her. Toni's family consisted of her mother, her two older brothers, Don and Terry, her older sister Janice, her younger sister Bonnie and two younger brothers, Bud and Greg (nicknamed Peanut). Little did I know I would become a member of this family someday.

I was still living with my aunt and uncle at the time I met Toni. I don't think my aunt and uncle could handle my situation with them much longer. I was away from the house a lot and still arriving back home at an hour that was unacceptable to them.

My uncle found out who I was seeing, and, to my amazement, thought Toni was the reason for my being out so late at nights! He went to see Toni's mother to talk with her about her daughter and find out why she could stay out so late at night. My future mother-in-law, Mabel, advised my uncle that Toni was always home at the time she was told to be home. She was quite disturbed by my uncle's behavior, and she made it known to him.

I was with Toni every moment I could. My friend Kenny and I would meet after school and drive over to see Toni and Bonnie almost every day. We would hang out and maybe drive around or get a bite to eat.

Toni's older brother let us use his brand-new '57 Chevy for the entire weekend. It was a black convertible and very fast. We did a lot of driving around with the top down. Kenny drove all the time since I did not have a license. Toni's brothers were great to me and did not mind that I was dating their sister. The whole Brown family felt like a family to me, and I loved all of them. Little did I know at the time that I would spend my entire life with Toni and them.

One time, after school, Kenny and I wanted to see the girls before we went to an away football game. We jumped in Kenny's Ford and went to see them. We stayed until the last minute and left in a hurry, as we were going to be late for the bus leaving with the other players. We pulled into Riverside High School and saw the bus with the players ready to depart the school grounds. We were yelled at by the coach to get our uniforms and get on the bus. The coach was quite mad, and we both sat on the bench for most of the football game.

Every moment I was not with Toni, she was all I thought about. I certainly did not know much about love, but I did know that what I wanted was to be with her. I could talk with her and share my deepest thoughts with her. She also confided in me about her family, and about how much she missed her dad. Toni and I had both lost our fathers. Even though I hardly knew mine, we both suffered from a lack of a father during the difficult teenage years. I believe that brought us closer together.

UPROOTED AGAIN

November 8, 1956, is another day I will never forget. I was in class at Riverside High School when I was summoned to the office where a social worker, Mrs. Green, was waiting for me. Mrs. Green advised me that I would no longer be attending Riverside High School and would be leaving with her. She escorted me to her car, which was packed with my clothes and personal items. I recall telling her that I would go with her, but I would not be staying with her. I had to be back for our last football game of the season, which I was to play at Riverside.

She took me to a place in Cleveland to stay overnight since there was nowhere else to go. She went inside with me, checked me in and left. As I recall, it was a place for smaller children. I felt sick at heart, like I was right back where I'd started.

One of the smaller boys told me about a door that was always left open, and that I would be able to leave when the attendant was not covering the exit. The day of the big game, I sneaked out, hopped on a bus and returned to Riverside High School. I arrived just prior to the game starting and found my friends and the coach. I asked the coach if I could play in the game, but he explained to me that the police were looking for me as a runaway and that would not be possible. I understood his decision, but I desperately wanted to play. Frustrated, angry and sad, I hung out in a friend's car for the rest of the evening until the game was over.

After the game ended, my friend Tom Johnson came over to the car and talked to me. He must have talked to his dad about my situation because he invited me to go home with him. I climbed out of the car, and Tommy and I left for his house.

Mr. Johnson was a very distinguished gentleman with a full head of white hair and a white mustache. He and Mrs. Johnson sat down and talked to me about returning to the home in the morning, and then, to my astonishment, asked me if I would like to come and live with them and their family. I readily agreed to return to the children's home with him, as he promised he would get me out as soon as possible.

I liked him and his wife after being with them a short time. Later in life, when I matured a little and realized what they had done for me, I was able to thank them, in a proper way, in person. When you are young and ignorant, you don't think as an adult, but I am forever grateful for the chance to have lived with them and live as a real family. I wish that every boy and girl in the orphanage would have had the good fortune I had to live with people like Johnsons.

I stayed with the Johnson family on the night of November 9. Their son, Tom, played on the football team and was also a senior that year at Riverside. On the morning of November 10, when Mr. Johnson found out that I had run away from the receiving home, he talked with me and returned me to the receiving home that afternoon. I accepted their offer to live with them and continue at Riverside. I believed that I could talk things over with the Johnsons. The Johnsons' home was investigated by the welfare office, and it seemed it was worth a trial for me to be placed there. The ability to do good schoolwork and to live in a good home and attend college was also possible. I found out that I could remain with the Johnsons in Painesville if I accepted the reasonable rules of the family. Mr. Johnson advised me that it may take some time before arrangements could be made to live with him. He promised me that I would be living with them eventually, but before that, I was sent to the

Cleveland Detention Home for older boys. I was not too happy to be there, to put it mildly.

DETENTION HOME

My first day at the Detention Home while getting in line to eat, I was looking for a place to sit down and ended up sitting with an all-black table. While positioning my chair, I bumped a black male with my chair. A fight started with him being the aggressor, calling me a name and saying words to the effect, "Say excuse me, you motherfucker!" I hit him right away, the guards came flying in, and we were taken down to the basement. As I recall, the guard made us put on boxing gloves. I got the best of this fight. We were sent back to our rooms afterwards.

Once, I was taking a shower in a large shower room when a black male was struck in the back with a bar of soap with a razor blade in the soap. There was a lot of blood in the shower, as it turned red quickly. I must admit that I was scared and could not understand why I was sent to this place. During the first night in my bed, I observed another male climb into the bed across from me. I slept with my eyes open the whole time I was in that place.

There was a room called the day room where we spent leisure time when nothing else was going on. A big fight started in the room, and all I recall is that the room was full of guards who were tossing guys around as I was hiding under a table watching the action. I think the blacks in the room were coming for me for beating up the guy the day before with the boxing gloves.

The guards began to watch over me after they found out that I did not commit a crime for which I was in the detention center. I would work with the staff doing chores around the buildings, like mopping floors and

Dormitory in the Cleveland Detention Home

cleaning. I also attended some sort of classes while at the center. As I recall, some of the guys did not even know the alphabet. I did not have to attend the classes awfully long, and instead, I did the cleaning work.

One late night while I lay in bed with my eyes open, I heard a voice say, "Give me your sheets." I felt cold air, as if someone had opened a window. I realized some of the guys in the center of the room were going to jump out of the window, which I believe was the second- or third-story window. The windows had a wire mesh over them, and I believe they had pried the lock open and opened the wire screening on the window. I could hear them preparing to jump out. I heard the sheets tear and a thump when a person hit the ground. I believe about five or six guys were able to break out of the detention home that evening.

I was pretty much scared the whole time I was there, which I believe was three days or so. I believe when the guys jumped out the window that night it made the television news in Cleveland. While lying in bed that night, I thought I would never do anything wrong to be placed in prison. I do not remember any more incidents about the detention center except that I was finally able to leave to live with the Johnson family.

Today, at seventy-nine years of age, when I look back at my life, I feel the hand of God has been on my shoulders guiding me in all the ventures I have undertaken.

The date that I was in the detention home was on, or about, November 13, 1956. I was placed in the Johnson home on November 18, 1956, in Painesville, Ohio.

My brother Tony, meanwhile, was placed with a maternal aunt when we both left Parmadale in 1952. After three months, my aunt and uncle requested that Tony be removed from their home. Our social worker took him from school one day and drove him to a foster home with a family in Middleburgh Heights while I was staying with the Johnson family. I did not know where my sisters currently were.

LIFE WITH THE JOHNSONS

My life with the Johnson family could not have been better. Tommy and I were good friends, played on the football team and hung out together. Mr. and Mrs. Johnson were two of the finest parents any child could have. I did not realize what they had done for me, including all the love and caring they showed me, until later in life as I matured. I was quite happy living with them. I do not believe I was ever in any serious trouble while staying with them.

Toni's mom, Mabel, was a great lady. I honestly believe that she liked me from the time I first met her until she died. Mabel treated me as if I were her own son, but she was quite strict about her daughter being home at a reasonable hour. Many times when I would bring Toni home after a night out, Kenny and I would go into the house and stay for quite a while until Mabel said it was time to leave. One evening Toni and I were downstairs in the living room when Mabel shouted from the upstairs bedroom that it was time to leave. Well, at the bottom of the stairs I replied, "Good night Mrs. Calabash, wherever you are." This was a saying from the old Jimmy Durante show, which he said at the closing of his television show. I said it to Mabel in the same type of raspy voice that Jimmy Durante used in signing off the air. I could hear her upstairs laughing to herself.

Toni had two younger brothers living at home, along with her sister Bonnie. Toni and Bonnie had the responsibility to care for the younger boys when Mabel was working. Mabel worked extremely hard to support herself and her kids after losing her husband, Bob. Mabel worked at the Mentor school and as a cook at Kenny King's restaurant. Mabel worked long hours but hardly ever complained. When her husband Bob died, she had the full burden of raising her children. She did a fantastic job. Bonnie and Toni cooked for the younger boys and kept the house clean and babysat for the two of them. I enjoyed the home atmosphere and spent much of my time at the house. The older boys, Terry and Don, were both married, and their sister Janice was also married. Mabel had a total of seven children.

It was still late 1956, and I seemed to adjust very well while at the Johnson home, as it was a great family to be with. I do not recall any serious problems I had in school or any disciplinary situations at home. Tommy and I were good buddies and got along very well, as I spent a lot of time with him. I spent more time with Toni and her family. When I was not in school, I would be at Toni's house. She watched over her two younger brothers, as Mabel was working two jobs as a cook at the school and a cook at a local eatery. I remember she would arrive home late evening quite exhausted. My main desire in life, at that moment, was to be with Toni. My interest in school was the high school band and the football team where I played halfback.

One day at school, I was in the parking lot smoking a cigarette with a friend in his car. I do not recall who it was that called the assistant principal, but I was taken to his office and suspended from school for three days. I was told to advise Mr. and Mrs. Johnson about the violation. Smoking was not the thing to do. When I arrived home in the late afternoon, I did not have the courage to tell Mr. and Mrs. Johnson about the three-day suspension. I went to bed that night and still had not told them. But the next morning, while sitting around the breakfast table, I was incredibly quiet. I knew I had to tell them, as it was time to leave for school. I finally got the courage to tell them both. Mr. Johnson nonchalantly told me not to worry. He said, "You can help me out the next three days working on installing windows." I was able to be with him for three days.

He was quite a person; no, not quite a person, he was a great man who laughed a lot and was fun to be with. One day Tommy and I went with his dad to help him install windows in Ashtabula, Ohio. We arrived at the house and noticed a lot of women looking out the window as we approached. Something was different, but I did not know until later that it was a house of prostitution. Tommy and I laughed till we hurt. What a day!

I'm sure during my stay with the Johnsons that I had to adhere to the rules and curfews. In juvenile court in Cleveland, before the judge released me to Mr. Johnson, the judge advised him that my curfew during school days was to be nine pm. Mr. Johnson stated to the judge that I would be treated the same as his son, as the curfew for him is ten pm. The judge agreed with Mr. Johnson.

MUSIC AND SCHOOL LIFE

I still played my clarinet and sax quite a bit and practiced with our newly formed group called The Aristocrats. We were progressing well with playing rock 'n' roll and slow dance music. We played "Rock Around the Clock," as Bill Haley and the Comets were popular, other songs, and sang all our parts. It was fantastic when the kids would clap for us. We all loved it, as Bill Haley and the Comets were our favorite group. I must be truthful about playing with the band. We were drinking beer while we played, but I do not ever recall getting into trouble over it, as there was a lot of underage smoking and drinking during those early years. I never did drugs, and everyone I hung out with never did drugs.

I remember one time being with another high school friend who drove to the Manners restaurant to buy some funny tobacco. I didn't know what he meant. I do not know if he connected with the person, as I never saw anyone smoking pot that I hung around with, but we did drink our share of beer.

Mrs. Johnson would have her friends over to the house and always asked me to play the clarinet or sax for them. I played for her, and it was obvious to me she sincerely loved it. Her eyes sparkled with pride.

DATING: GETTING MORE SERIOUS WITH TONI

Tommy would take his girlfriend, Joan, and I would take Toni on double dates to the movies. A movie called *Cat on a Hot Tin Roof* was playing at the Chardon Theater, and we all went together. I don't recall too much about the movie, but it may have had a little sex in it, as several guys our age were sitting behind us using foul language.

Now, Tommy did not stand for any of the language they were using in front of our girls, and the rest of the patrons were not enjoying it either. I don't know why the ushers didn't throw them out, but I would look over at Tommy during the funny part of the movie, and he wasn't laughing. The movie ended, Tommy stood up, reached over the seat, and hit the first kid in the nose, and I am quite sure the guy's nose was broken. I began to pound on the other guy as he was seated. The lights turned on in the theater as most of the patrons were watching us. If I remember correctly, they were clapping. Both of our girls were very frightened, and we began walking fast for the door to make our getaway. We entered the car and left town in a hurry when we heard the sirens heading for the theater.

We made it home with no trouble, but the next day in the local paper there was an article about a small riot at the Chardon Theater. I remember the boy's remarks in the paper saying that we started the fight for no reason. Maybe they did not use foul language like that for a while.

Kenny and I would drive to Bonnie and Toni's house almost every day after school, as I wanted to be with Toni all the time. We would talk about her recently deceased father and how much she missed him. We talked a lot together about almost anything. There was something happening between us that I might not have fully understood at fifteen or sixteen years old. I needed her to be with me always and thought about her when I was away from her. We may have met and stayed together for the simple reason she needed someone and I needed her.

It was in 1957 that my life would dramatically change forever. Toni and I had been seeing one another for a little over a year, and I must admit I was very naive about sexual matters. Being only sixteen years old, I didn't know Jack shit. No adult had ever sat down and talked to me about the birds and bees, so I learned from other teenagers, who were as naive as I was. This story must continue and be told as I experienced it.

I believe it was sometime in September 1956 that Toni discovered she was pregnant. Toni eventually told her mother. I do not remember how I was able to advise Mr. and Mrs. Johnson about the pregnancy. They, in turn, being my guardians, had to advise the County Welfare Department, and a meeting occurred at the Johnson family home with my caseworker, Mrs. Green. Toni was eighteen years old at the time and would turn nineteen in February 1958. I was sixteen years old and would turn seventeen on October 13, 1957.

While in the living room discussing matters with the family and the caseworker, I was advised by the caseworker that I did not have to marry Toni and could walk away from the situation. I answered the caseworker immediately of my intentions without any hesitation. I will marry Toni, and that was my final decision. Would I not be free from the welfare department and be able to manage my own life, make my own decisions, have my own family and decide which way my life will lead me? If I could be in charge, would I be able to have my brother live with me? The meeting was adjourned.

It was only weeks later that it was decided the welfare department would give my future mother-in-law custody of me until I reach my eighteenth birthday. My future mother-in-law was now my legal guardian. WOW! I began, in earnest, to look for a job. I filled out an application at a Kroger store at the Painesville shopping center for a grocery clerk position. I told the manager that I desperately needed the job, as I was going to be married and would be raising a child. I was soon notified that I had the position.

On October 5, 1957, Toni and I were married in Lyndhurst, Ohio, by a justice of the peace. My new mother-in-law and guardian had purchased a sport coat for me to wear, as I did not have a dime in my pocket. We were married on a Sunday, and while leaving the ceremony, we were peppered with rice as we left the justice of the peace's office. I remember how we both laughed as we headed for the car. My new sister-in-law was with us, and her boyfriend Kenny drove us home. My new wife Toni and I arrived home at my mother-in-law's house where a small party was held for us.

Toni's two older brothers, two younger brothers, and two sisters were also home. Later in the evening as we entered our small bedroom to retire for the evening, we had quite a surprise. Toni's older brothers had rigged our small bed to cave in as we climbed into it; they were all heard laughing in the other room when our bed collapsed. I had to go to sleep, as my new job started in the morning.

FIRST JOB

I reported the next day for my first day of full-time work as a grocery clerk. I was assigned to the head grocery clerk for instructions. I unloaded grocery trucks, packed groceries at the checkout counter when the lines were full of customers, swept floors, returned shopping carts from the parking lot and other duties that the head clerk ordered. I would refill the grocery shelves, as the items would sell, and observed what items sold the best. I dusted shelves as needed and kept my assigned aisles stocked as items would sell. I remember my first paycheck for a forty-hour work week was $80 net.

Life at my mother-in-law's house was pleasant as Toni kept up with the housework and cooking. She also watched her two younger brothers during the day as her mom worked at the high school and at a local restaurant in the evening. Toni would drive me to work at the grocery store in her mom's car and pick me up in the evening.

On the weekends, the two young boys, with Toni and I, would go to a local drive-in movie theater. Toni and I helped a lot with the daily chores around the house so that when Toni's mom would return home in the evening things would be clean. The whole family would eat together and watch television in the evening. I helped pay for the weekly groceries and contributed to the household expenses.

Some evenings, Toni and I would take the young boys to the restaurant where my mother-in-law worked. I felt like I was now in charge of my life and not in the control of the welfare department. My mother-in-law was my legal guardian, but I was able to make my own decisions, and I don't believe I ever disappointed her.

After six months or so, while at the store, I was able to work without supervision and took pride in my assigned area of responsibility. I began to order all the items I was responsible for and maintain proper inventory so the bestselling items were not out of stock. I was in the grocery clerk union and was paid union wages. We all wore clean aprons, white shirts and blue bowties while working on the floor. The store was meticulously clean, and the shelves were dusted regularly. I enjoyed talking to customers, helping them find items in the store as they shopped, and would try to order items that we normally did not stock.

I do remember that one of my wife's classmates came to the house. Chuck was a very likable guy and we had become friends of sort, as Chuck was dating a friend of my wife's. We were discussing our situation with Chuck about not having our own vehicle, and Chuck told me that he had an old Plymouth that he was trying to get rid of. He was going to junk it and asked me if I would want the car, as it was drivable. I was not able to say no and accepted his offer. The vehicle was a blue 1952 Plymouth. I was so proud to have a vehicle; I began to clean it outside. I didn't care that it was snowing, and when I cleaned the snow off the car, it appeared to have been painted with a broom. I did not care; I was so happy to have a car to drive to work, and it was free. We would soon purchase our second car, which was a 1952 Chevrolet.

I should say that the store manager, Jay Sanders, treated me like a son. He was a great person and did help me while I was employed at the store. Mr. Sanders was quite pleased with the way I worked and handled myself in the store. I looked up to him as a father figure, as he treated me so well. I was happy to be working with him and I thought a great deal of him.

OUR SON IS BORN

The big moment in our life came on May 8, 1958, when my son Robert was born into the world. It was Mother's Day, and Toni was the youngest mother in the hospital that day. Toni's picture holding our son was published in the local paper, the Painesville Telegraph. Toni looked so happy, and I was so proud of her holding our newborn son. I cannot describe how I felt when I was able to hold him in my arms. We were so happy, and I was the proud father of my own son.

Toni soon became the best mother a child could have. I had the best wife a man could ever hope for. We had our moments but always managed to survive our problems, as I tried as hard as I could to be a good father and husband. There were times I stayed out late with my friends and partied with them while Toni stayed home caring for her brothers and our son. I regretted my shortcomings the next day and would sheepishly ask forgiveness from Toni. Toni's mom always stuck up for me and reminded Toni that I was sowing my wild oats and reminded Toni, at times, my age and the responsibilities I had. At seventeen years old, I never missed work because of the late hours I spent out at times, nor did I miss work for calling in sick.

I loved my mother-in-law who always spoke highly of me to others. Of course, I hurt when I caused the love of my life to hurt. I felt guilty that I could not say "no" to my friends when they asked me to go out with them. I was a married man, and when I did go out, I did have a lot of laughs and drank a lot of beer. I still played out with our band for a short time after I was married. The band eventually broke up as we all went in different directions. It was great fun while it lasted.

MY BROTHER TONY

As I wrote earlier, my younger brother Tony had been placed into a foster home with Aunt Claire when we left the orphanage, and then after three months, he was unceremoniously moved to a second foster home in Middleburgh Heights. He stayed there until he was fifteen years old and a sophomore at St. Ignatius High School in Cleveland.

It was in 1958 that I was informed that Tony was removed from that home and placed on a Greyhound bus bound for Boys Town, Nebraska. Toni and I were terribly upset and tried to have my brother come to live with us. That did not go anywhere, probably due to our immaturity and the fact that Toni and I were starting our own family.

We stayed in touch with Tony by sending him things he needed and writing him letters.

Tony stayed at Boys Town for almost a year when he came back to Cleveland and was placed in St. Anthony's Home for Boys on Detroit Avenue. St. Ignatius High School took him back, thankfully. We were able to see each other occasionally, even though it was quite a way from the west side to Painesville.

FINDING MY LITTLE SISTER LINDA

My two little sisters, Linda and Carol, were taken into the adoption/ foster care system after our mother died. I was old enough to remember them and often wondered where they ended up. I was only seventeen and married with a child, but I could not ignore my desire to find my sisters.

As is the norm, their whereabouts were not public knowledge. I knew where my brother lived and was able to contact him and occasionally see him, but my sister's location was unknown to me. I do not remember how I finally found Linda, but I did. Linda had been adopted by a family that lived not far from us.

I called the family and explained who I was and that I wanted to see my sister. Linda's adoptive parents were understandably cautious and not wild about the idea, but finally relented and agreed that Toni and I could show up as "friends of the family" and visit.

Today Linda describes the visit: *When I first met my brother Karl, I was about twelve years old. My mother told me that a couple from Painesville wanted to meet me and said they were friends of the family. I thought that was strange! Why would they want to meet me, and if they were friends of the family living so close, why haven't I met them before? When they arrived, my mom stayed in the kitchen instead of coming into the living room.*

When I saw Karl, I immediately felt that I knew him, as he kept watching me and not saying much. I thought, could this be my brother? I thought he would say so if he was, but he didn't. When they left, I still had a funny feeling that I really knew him from somewhere. I asked my mother again who they were and why they wanted to meet me, but she never answered and didn't say another word about it. I didn't see them again until many years later.

Toni and I left Linda's home with mixed emotions. We could not really establish a family relationship with my sister and her adoptive parents. However, we had found her, got to see her, and left knowing that she had a good home with loving adoptive parents. We would have to be content with that.

My other sister's whereabouts, Carol, would not be discovered until much later.

PROMOTION AT THE STORE

Eventually my position as a grocery clerk led me to having an interest in working in the meat department. A friend of the family was employed as a meat cutter in the store where I was employed. He sparked my interest to learn a trade and become a member of the meat cutter's union. I started coming to work on my days off from the grocery clerk position to learn the trade. I was not paid, but I had an interest in becoming a journeyman meat cutter.

I was transferred to the meat department as an apprentice meat cutter. After working as a grocery clerk, I received a little more pay as an apprentice and joined the meat cutter union, called the Amalgamated Meat Cutters and Butcher Workmen of Northern America. I never did know what 'amalgamated' meant and never did ask, but it sounded impressive.

It wasn't long before I became a journeyman meat cutter. An Italian friend of my uncle's, Frank, was a big help in the learning process. We used to tease him a lot when he started dating a woman he was interested in. When he had a date with her, we would ask him if he were "getting any" and he would angrily reply, "Mind your own business," but he would laugh a short time later. One time a grouchy lady wanted a chunk of baloney that was on sale, and Frank showed the tube of baloney to the lady. She angrily stated, "I don't want any from the beginning," and with that comment, Frank turned the tube of baloney around and said, "Okay, how about some from the end?" The angry lady left the store.

The same lady came in several weeks later when chuck roast was on sale for $0.39 a pound. Frank politely showed the lady a nice cut of meat, and she angrily said, "That kind of meat had too much bone." Frank started to walk behind the counter wearing his bloody apron and hat. He started walking like a cow with no bones and said to her, "Lady, how in the hell can a cow walk with no bones?" This customer walked out of the store again.

Within a year or so, I was promoted to Meat Manager of the oldest store in the company. I was the youngest meat manager in the company as I remember. I did well as Meat Manager in the oldest store in the division and was soon promoted to a larger, more modern store. I was beginning to be bored with the meat business, but I was being paid a decent wage and supported my family.

Another opportunity arose for me when another store close by was being remodeled. I was promoted to run the meat department, which was the most modern meat department in the division. I remember leaving the house one morning to go to work as a meat cutter, and I was driving to work and had stopped at a stop sign. I thought I had to relieve myself of some gas, and I moved up in the seat to let the gas escape. Well, it wasn't gas at all. I had pooped my pants. I turned around and returned home to my mother-in-law's house. As I walked in the door with my legs sort of far apart, my mother-in-law was sitting in the living room and asked me what was wrong. I replied sort of giggling that I had shit my pants. She started laughing and could not stop for several minutes. I went and got cleaned up and returned to work a little bit late.

While I was the meat manager, the whole idea of working in the store the rest of my life became a little difficult for me to realize. I began taking flying lessons at the local airport around 1965. The crew

I was responsible for in the meat department and I began throwing quarters against the wall and gambling which quarter would be closest to the wall. We began drinking beer while playing the quarter game. Things were getting out of hand, as we were buzzed a great deal of the time. I was to blame for allowing this activity to take place.

DAUGHTER CONNIE IS BORN

Our daughter Connie was born in January 1960. Toni was home taking care of our son and daughter. This was a happy time for us at home and incredibly happy time for my wife. Toni loved our children and was probably the best mother that they could ever have, as well as the best wife a man could ever have. When Toni wanted to use the '52 Chevy during the day, she would drive me to work.

However, there were some rumblings of trouble on the horizon: Toni did not appreciate the drinking that was going on at my workplace and had admonished me about it numerous times. Toni's father had been an alcoholic, and she was fearful of my going down that same road. She made her feelings known about the drinking my buddies and I were doing at work. If I had two bottles of beer, she would smell it on me.

THE HAIRPIECE

One day, Toni and I were in downtown Cleveland for some reason, walking through the stores, when she saw a sign advertising hairpieces. As we were walking by, she stopped and said let's go in and look at them. I thought she was crazy, but I went in. After a short time, the owner came out and took us to a display area. Since I had a receding hairline, I guess my wife was interested in getting me more hair. The gentleman came out with a hairpiece, placed it on my head, and brushed and combed it. After he was done, I turned around and looked at my wife. She said buy it! I laughed and thought she was kidding, but she was not. We didn't even ask the price; I bought the hairpiece for $850 to the best of my recollection. My wife thought it was sharp, and I laughed all the way home with the hairpiece on my head.

The next day I wore it to the store where I was an assistant manager. I was standing in the office with several cashiers looking at me, asking each other who is that guy? They did not recognize me at all, and I worked forty hours a week at the store. I had so much fun with that hairpiece. At times, I would go to a bar and have a few beers. I would loosen up the tape that held hairpiece on my head. Suddenly, after two or three beers, I would pretend I was going to sneeze, and I did a fake sneeze, causing the hairpiece to fly off and onto the bar. I wish I had a camera to take pictures of the patrons in the bar. My brother-in-law and I could not stop laughing, and everyone else had a good laugh. My wife couldn't believe what I had done, but she had a good laugh also.

During this time, I was also going to night school in Cleveland, Ohio to finish my education. I was working full-time at the grocery store and going to school two or three times a week, as I had to finish credit hours needed for my high school diploma from Riverside High. Also, during this time, I worked part-time at a gas station. Toni and I eventually left her home and moved into a small but nice apartment. We were now on our own.

My younger brother Tony graduated from High School in August of 1961. He was living on his own after leaving St. Anthony's Home for Boys when he turned eighteen. He and his buddy Duffy flipped a coin to decide if they were joining the Marines or the Navy. It came up Navy, and they immediately left for the Great Lakes Naval Training Center in Chicago to start boot camp.

DEATH OF COUSIN JACK

On September 30, 1961, my beloved cousin Jack was killed in a terrible motorcycle accident. He was only twenty-three years old. The family and everyone who knew him were devastated.

Jack had always liked to boat on Lake Erie where he and his friends would go water skiing and fishing. He had joined the Army Reserves when he was old enough.

Fifty years after his death, the *News Herald* published an article about how Jack's dog tags had turned up. The dog tags were found by a gentleman while walking his dog on the beach. The gentleman found the dog tags about ten feet from shore. The dog saw the tags because they were so shiny, so he had to check them out. Also on the chain was a sterling silver ring. My cousin Vince believed Jack lost his tags while water skiing or fishing in the lake. Vince believes the ring that was with the dog tags belonged to an ex-girlfriend. The gentleman who found the tags tracked down Vince, who was most grateful for the find.

I was working as a grocery clerk at a shopping center at the time of Jack's death. His death devastated me, as we were like brothers. A high school friend of mine, John Zuber, had died in an airplane crash in 1970 at the Cuyahoga County Airport. It was very sad to hear these two had died, especially my cousin Jack. Jack had a younger brother and sister and was the son of my aunt and uncle who first took me in when I left the orphanage. It was a very sad day. On top of it all, I was laid off from the airport now and had to find a new job.

A HOME OF OUR OWN

Toni called me one day and told me of a new house for sale on a half-acre lot. A three-bedroom ranch with an attached garage; she was extremely excited and wanted to go look at this house. I told her we had not saved enough to afford a house, and I was not yet twenty-one. Toni was twenty-one, though, and she made an appointment with the builders to talk to them about signing a contract. The house was on a quiet street and was a great place to raise our children. We were both excited about buying a house, but I did not have high hopes of getting a loan. The builder let us sign a contract to purchase the house, and we were both very excited when he let us move in.

Shortly after we moved into the house, the builder went bankrupt. We never heard a word from him or the bank he dealt with. We did not make any house payments. We lived in the house for about a year when the bank called us and asked if we would like to purchase it for $12,000. The payments would be $80 a month. I was shocked that we were able to buy this house. We jumped at the chance, signed the papers, and began our life in a new house. If it wasn't for Toni, we would not have had this home.

I decided to make the double-car attached garage into a large family room with help from Toni's brother, Terry. The room was finished and furnished. It was a great room, and the kids loved it. I believe Connie was about three or four years old when we acquired the ranch style home, and Bob was six years old or so.

When I was a grocery clerk and received my first paycheck of $80, I was invited to a poker game by one of Toni's classmates who I had become friends with. I knew a little bit of poker and walked out of the game with $160. I was hooked and began studying the game by reading books by the pros. Years later, when I moved to Alaska, I legally played for high stakes.

PILOT'S LICENSE – A DREAM COMES TRUE

I passed my private pilot's test in June 1965 and was a private pilot single engine land. I was ecstatic when I passed my first flight test. I was able to continue flying lessons and hung out a great deal at the local airport. I was able to accompany the commercial pilots on trips by sitting in the right seat of the aircraft. I learned a lot from the frequent trips I took, such as navigation and takeoff and landings during day and nighttime.

To build my flying time up for enough hours to obtain a

commercial license, I took trips to the Air Force Museum in Dayton with my friends. The friends would pay for the aircraft rental, and I would build up hours.

Sometimes I would fly right seat to the Indianapolis races with the chief pilot, whom I admired greatly. He was sort of a short fellow who smoked a cigar all the time. After parking the aircraft and getting the passengers safely off the plane, I would head into the raceway as well. The chief would stand under the stairway to the upper-level seats, smoking his cigar and staring at the women going up the stairway. From time to time he would call me over when he saw a lady wearing no underpants, but most of the time he just stood there by himself as I laughed at his antics.

Flying ultimately became my passion; it had been my dream as a little kid, and of course it was far more exciting than working at a grocery store. I was starting to believe that I could actually become a commercial pilot.

BROTHER TONY COMES HOME

In August of 1965, my brother Tony got his honorable discharge from the U.S. Navy in San Francisco. His last ship, the aircraft carrier USS Ticonderoga CVA14, had recently returned from service in the western Pacific and was in dry dock at Hunter's Point Naval Shipyard. It was great to have him home with us. He worked with me at the supermarket for a couple of months while he looked for work in his trade, electronic technician, that he learned in the Navy. I had Tony working in the meat department helping cut and wrap meat. We had some fun times until he got an interview with AT&T in downtown Cleveland. He was hired and moved into Cleveland to be close to work.

After a few months at AT&T, Tony was bored and unhappy with the work, so he answered an ad for technicians to work on the Air Force Eastern Missile Test Range. Tony took the test, was hired, and set out for Patrick AFB in Florida for intake and assignment. He was assigned to Grand Bahama Island where he worked in telemetry, tracking missile launches from submarines, and from Cape Kennedy. Tony has a certificate for serving in support of Apollo XI, the first moon landing.

As you will see later, Tony eventually ended up in Juneau, Alaska, in 1972 and was instrumental in my future career changes.

CHAPTER FOUR

THE FLYING MEAT CUTTER

WORKING AS A PILOT

I RECEIVED MY COMMERCIAL PILOT'S LICENSE on October 1966, my flight instructor certification in 1967, and my multi-engine license in 1968. I left the grocery store and my meat-cutting job in 1967 to begin my flying career as a full-time pilot at a local airport.

During my flying career, I was instructing and conducting air taxi operations to Cleveland Hopkins International Airport four or five times a day. The aircrafts I flew during my career were the Cessna 150, Cessna 172, Cessna 206 and Cessna 337 Sky Master. I spent many hours in the Lockheed 10 Electra, Cessna 402, and Cessna 310 flying as copilot. My next aircraft would have been the Cessna 310 that I would be qualified to fly as pilot if layoffs had not occurred.

I remember flying the Cessna 310 in the right seat at night when both the pilot and I saw something coming straight at us at high speed. We were heading home from a trip when suddenly something flew over us so fast, we could not tell what it was. We looked at each other and could not believe what we had just experienced. We were used to observing other aircrafts, but this was very unusual. We were tempted to call air traffic control to ask if they had anything on their radar that covered our area but chose not to do that and continued on our way. The chief pilot, who had much more experience than I did, was as amazed by what we had seen.

I was assigned my first female flying student who had won a contest prize of eight hours of flight instruction. Eight hours of primary instruction was about the average time for a new pilot to solo. She was doing well and soon it was time for her to solo. I was in the right seat while she was making several landings on her own. Two of the three landings that she made were terrible, but the key element was that she knew how to salvage the landings safely. I had her stop the plane at the end of the runway, and I got out. I watched her take off as I made the sign of the cross and prayed that she would make her solo landings safely. It was quite an experience for me being a new flight instructor. She did very well and accomplished three excellent landings with me out of the airplane. One of the times of most angst for a new flight instructor was when to get out and let the student go it alone.

The *Lake County Painesville Telegraph* reported on August 26, 1968, that on the previous day I served as copilot of a Lockheed Model 10 Electra operating out of Lost Nation Airport. The Lockheed Electra first flew in 1935, and Amelia Earhart flew one when she attempted to fly around the world in 1936. The Electra carries ten passengers and a crew of two. We were scheduled to leave early in the morning for a flight to Duquoin, Illinois, for the Hambletonian Stakes horse race. We refueled the airplane and performed the preflight checks, then we began loading the ten passengers and their baggage in preparation for takeoff. The pilot I

Amelia Earhart flew a Lockheed Electra 10 when she disappeared.

was flying with had seventeen thousand hours of total flying time but just twenty hours of time in the Lockheed 10, while I had close to thirty-five hours in the right seat.

We taxied out for takeoff on schedule. We completed the run-up of the two 450 horsepower engines and began to accelerate down the runway. As copilot, my responsibility was to keep the throttles full forward to prevent them from sliding back, thus reducing power and to keep eyes scanning the aircraft's instrument panel. Suddenly I felt the aircraft begin moving erratically and heading for the side of the runway—we were out of control. The Electra struck a dirt bank, collapsing the right landing gear, and caught fire. We immediately began to evacuate the aircraft. All ten passengers got out safely, followed by the pilot and me. There were several minor injuries suffered by passengers, but the Electra was a total loss. Painesville Township and Leroy Township fire departments responded and extinguished the blaze.

The next day I was scheduled to fly the first of several trips to Cleveland Hopkins Airport, as we were an air taxi operation. I was piloting a Cessna 206 aircraft with several passengers on board. Prior to takeoff, all passengers were discussing the previous day's crash of the Lockheed 10 as we were taxiing past the wreckage. The destroyed Lockheed was still smoldering, and all the seats were bare of upholstery. As we taxied by, I jokingly stated, "Good morning ladies and gentlemen. On the right side of the runway you will observe my first attempted takeoff!" I later learned that I was given the early flight by my boss so that I would be flying soon after the Lockheed 10 incident. His operating theory was the one about getting back on that horse. I was okay, as all passengers and crew survived the crash suffering only a few minor injuries.

On another charter flight, I was scheduled to fly some businessmen to an airstrip just north of Cincinnati. I was to fly as pilot in command of a single engine Cessna 206 with four or five passengers. The flight down was uneventful with good weather. After landing I asked the passengers to return to the airport before dark, as there were no lights on the runway.

Well, they did not make it back on time. I do not believe they were intoxicated, but they had clearly been drinking. I taxied the Cessna 206 onto the grass runway and took off bound for Cuyahoga County Airport, ten miles east of Cleveland. The weather was clear with good visibility, and it appeared to be a routine flight. My passengers were all nodding off when, suddenly, the engine shuddered for a few seconds. It felt like one or more of the engine cylinders were not firing. Scanning the gauges, I saw no indication of the cause, but it concerned me enough that I started looking for a place to land in case I lost the engine. The passengers must have sensed something was wrong, as they all stirred from their slumber.

The engine sounded normal within a few seconds, but it acted up again several minutes later. At this point I called Cleveland radar to advise them of my position and the problem I was having. They asked me what engine I was having a problem with, and I replied with the only engine. They asked me if I wanted to declare an emergency and proceed to Cleveland Hopkins Airport. I advised them that I could see Cuyahoga County Airport not too far off, and it was closer than Cleveland Hopkins. I wanted to be in contact with air traffic control in case I had to make an emergency landing on a highway or a field. All went well, and I let my passengers off after landing safely at the Cuyahoga County Airport.

I flew the short trip back to our home field at Casement Airport in Painesville, Ohio, where I filed a report for the mechanics. I then drove home to relax and consider whether flying was the right occupation for me.

I was employed at the local airport from November 1967 to June 1970 when I, and others, were laid off. I attempted to get a position with a large airline, but the airlines were hiring mostly veterans.

I tried during the Vietnam War to enlist, as I was an experienced commercial pilot. I don't recall the exact year, but I and another pilot with more experience tried to join. I recall that it was with an army recruiter in mid-1968 when I was working as a commercial pilot. He spoke of us becoming warrant officers, but then asked both of us how many dependents we had. My friend had five dependents, and I had three. We were not accepted.

MARRIED LIFE AND BACK TO THE GROCERY BUSINESS

Toni and I were incredibly happy in our new home in a wonderful neighborhood to raise children. Toni was a great mother, having been raised in a large family, and being the fourth of seven, she knew very well how to run a home. Toni took charge of the younger children, Bonnie, brother Bud, and younger brother Peanut. Toni was a great cook and homemaker.

With my experience in the grocery business, I managed to acquire a job in 1970 as assistant manager with BI-RITE foods at a store in Northeastern Ohio. The store owner, Frank, was a great man whom I grew to admire. He knew I was young, newly married and very experienced in the business. During my time with him, I learned to love him as a father figure. He treated me very well, and I worked hard to learn the business while working for him. Frank loved the horse races and left the store early most of the time to attend them. He gambled heavily and was often successful. He treated me as if I were his own son and made a difference in my life. He was going to the races one day when I asked him to place a small bet on the daily double for me with the numbers one and three and three and one. The next day he came to the store with $600 for me! I won the daily double.

A Cessna 150 trainer.

I was soon doing all the ordering for the store as well as taking on more responsibility for daily operations. Frank told me that instead of a raise, he would allow me to "shop" after I closed the store, and to take whatever I needed. Toni would join me, and we loaded up with the best food, drink, and whatever other household items we needed.

The men working in the meat department loved to drink and did so often while working. They would frequently invite me and the head cashier/manager to the back room of the meat department for a drink. The meat manager was of Italian descent and boxed when he was younger. He was what you might call a "bad-ass."

One day the boys in the meat department caught a shoplifter and took the him to the back of the store where they beat the hell out of him. I thought they were going to beat him to death, and I got them to stop.

Toni was happy that I was back working in the grocery business again. I was home at a reasonable time and not flying all over the country.

I enjoyed working at BI-RITE foods but could not imagine doing this type of work for the rest of my life. I had to make a change. An opportunity arose for me to purchase a convenience food store in Richmond Heights, Ohio. Two friends of mine who worked with me in my early years at Kroger owned the store. They were both very successful in Painesville, Ohio, where they owned another convenience store. The convenience store for sale that they had purchased and owned for five years was always in the red. Thanks to them knowing me and my experience level, they let me purchase the store from them. I do not recall the details or the price that I paid, but I believe it was $50,000 lock, stock and barrel. The inventory and equipment were worth at least $50,000 on their own, so this was a bargain. This store was a franchise store and owned by Lockie Lee Dairy in Painesville, Ohio. I took over the store, and in the first month had the store in the black. I knew that I had to make this store successful.

At times, my wife and young son would help me and work in the store. I was concerned at times with leaving them alone, especially at nighttime. I learned not to leave them at nighttime at all because convenience stores nearby were robbed several times. At night I would normally be at the store 99 percent of the time, and I was always armed. One day I was having lunch with a friend when he advised me that someone was in the store; a man was attempting to steal a carton of cigarettes. Not one carton, but the whole case. We were having lunch next door when I ran back to the store, drew my weapon, and walked the man out of my store and called the police. He was stopped nearby in his car with a trunk load of groceries that he had stolen from another store.

I had a meat case where if someone needed help they would ring a bell. One day, I happened to be in my small office when I heard the bell ringing. I closed the office door but did not lock it. I went to the meat case to wait on a customer who was asking me questions about some of the meat that I had for sale. I felt funny or suspicious that she was kind of asking me questions and attempting to tie me up to keep me busy. Suddenly, I heard my metallic safe close, as the walls were concrete blocks. I drew my weapon, ran to the back of the store to my office and saw a man running toward the exit. The female was not far behind. I wanted to shoot him, but I could not see who might have been walking into the store.

I did not shoot. I don't recall how much money was taken. I then made it a point not to have my family working at night. When they were working, even in the daytime, I was normally there. The cashiers were told that if anyone came in to rob the store to give them whatever they wanted, including all the money.

I worked long hours at the store and even had a bunk placed in the back room. When I first purchased the store, I spent approximately eighteen hours a day there. My wife was not too happy when I stayed at the store, but I was too tired to drive home. The store closed at midnight, and I had to open in the morning. I arranged the entire store differently, kept the floors clean and maintained everything in working order. Having been a meat cutter, I kept a fresh meat case and fresh produce. The franchise holders were very pleased with the way the store looked after three to six months. The floors were always scrubbed, and the windows were always clean. The store was well stocked. I was getting to know a lot of my customers. It seemed like a very good life for our family. As the business started to improve, I decided to take on a partner, my brother-in-law Terry.

Toni liked to work at the store and would prefer working in the deli department. My son Bob was fifteen when I purchased the store, and my daughter Connie was thirteen. Both of them were beginning to be rebellious as teenagers; my son in particular was hanging around with a boy I did not like. I worried how my kids would turn out.

This was about the time that I was beginning to question our future. We wanted to get both of my children away from the environment here that I did not like. Toni and I really believed that Bob would be in a lot of trouble with the boy that he looked up to. That boy eventually wound up in prison. I was certain my son was smoking pot and drinking. One day while looking in his bedroom, I discovered a marijuana joint in one of his dresser drawers. Having never smoked pot, I lit the joint up, took one drag and started coughing. I put the joint out and never smoked another one.

Toni and I began talking about leaving Ohio and taking the kids to Alaska. My brother, Tony, had moved to Juneau in January of 1972 with his fiancé, Annette. They had been living in the Bahama Islands where they first met. After his discharge from the Navy, Tony took a job in the Bahamas as a technician tracking missile launches from submarines and from Cape Kennedy. After being laid off the tracking job, he stayed on the island working as a flight instructor/charter pilot. Tony had taken a leave of absence from his job to attend flight school in Fort Lauderdale, using the GI bill to pay for his lessons. Annette had moved to Freeport, Grand Bahama Island as a kid where her father worked in the construction industry. They eventually left the Bahamas due to the problems the Islands were going through as the young nation completed its independence from Great Britain. There were some difficulties that independence caused for foreign residents. Tony had a best friend from Alaska who had recruited him for a telephone technician job in Juneau, Alaska's capitol city.

Toni and I traveled to Juneau to visit them in 1973. I was totally in love with the place. Located in Southeast Alaska, Juneau is surrounded by forest, glaciers, mountains, and water. There is no way in or out except by boat or airplane. Fishing right offshore for salmon and halibut was world class. You could leave Juneau harbor in a small boat, and within minutes you would be in the wilderness. I went to Juneau to check out the job situation.

CHAPTER FIVE

NORTH TO ALASKA

After returning to Ohio, we decided that moving to Alaska was the right choice for us. Shortly afterwards, Bob and I went to Juneau to look for work and find a place to live. Toni and Connie planned to come north after we were settled.

Bob and Connie and Toni were not happy about leaving Ohio. My family had never lived anywhere but Mentor, Ohio, and now that we were leaving, they were all regretful. This was not a good sign.

Mabel Brown, my mother-in-law, had given me a big hug before we left home and said something to me that I will never forget: "You were more of a man at sixteen than most men that I know, and I have no worries about you taking my daughter and your children to Alaska." She had confidence in me, and I always respected her for feeling the way she did about me.

I think she knew that I had decided to remove my children from the negative environment that they had had in Ohio. Toni and I both realized that the move was designed to get our children "back on track," so to speak. Even so, Toni was depressed about leaving Ohio.

We arrived in Juneau and stayed with my brother Tony and his wife. It didn't take much time to find work; Juneau was booming at the time because of the Trans-Alaska Pipeline project.

A large new grocery store called Mark & Pac was opening in Juneau, and it was my best bet for immediate employment. I spoke with the manager and gave him my background in the grocery business. After talking with him, he was quite impressed and said that I had more experience than both he and his assistant manager. I was given the job and told a starting date based upon my return to Juneau with my family. I was very excited to find a job so quickly; I hadn't been in Alaska for more than a few days.

I found a double-wide trailer selling for $14,000 that was for sale in the adult section of a trailer park called Switzer Village. The back view out the trailer was of the mountains, and the front view was of the tidal flats in Gastineau Channel. We planned to live in Switzer Village until we found a suitable house to purchase. My son and I returned to Ohio to finalize our departure.

Back in Mentor, Ohio, I purchased a brand-new Chevrolet sports van and loaded it with all our personal items. We were on our way to a new life—me, Toni, Bob, Connie and our dog Lady. The drive to Alaska was immensely enjoyable to me and Lady, but the family was not as excited as I was about starting our new life in Alaska. It was a big move for all of us, but later in life, my son Bob and daughter Connie said that they felt I had done the right thing. They were both grateful to have the experience. My son Bob admitted to me that if we had not moved to Alaska, he might have been in jail because of his so-called friend always getting in serious trouble.

EARLY DAYS: NEAR DISASTER

Our first day in Juneau, Alaska, was a near disaster. Our two children Bob, seventeen, and Connie, fifteen, left in our new van to check out our new city. They ended up in a bar and began drinking; both were underage, but there were other young people in the bar who began drinking with them. Afterwards, Bob and Connie left the bar and began to drive the van toward home. Bob went to turn around in a driveway, but he was inebriated and not paying attention and failed to notice a patch of freshly poured concrete. The homeowner came out of the house with a shotgun, and, needless to say, he was very upset. Bob floored it and fled the scene.

While driving away, my son picked up two hitchhikers and discussed smoking some hash and drinking some more. While driving southbound on Thane Road, Bob rolled the van. No one was injured, so the two hitchhikers took off from the scene of the crash. My son and daughter were exiting the van when my son burned his hands badly on the hot exhaust pipes. The police arrived, and my daughter did not tell the truth about how the accident had happened and said that a car had run them off the road. My daughter, Connie, punched one of the officers in the throat after the officer began choking her brother Bob. Both my son and daughter ran from the police officers but were caught and taken to jail.

My new, paid-for Chevy sports van appeared to be a total wreck. It was a sad day for my wife and me, but on the other hand, both son and daughter may have been killed or killed some innocent person. We thank God above for sparing their lives on this first day in their new environment.

Another serious incident occurred shortly after the first. My daughter was not home, and my wife asked me to go out and look for her. I searched the downtown Juneau area for an hour, and finally found my daughter in another downtown bar. There she was sitting at the bar, legs crossed, drinking a beer. Next to her was a known drug dealer. A scuffle ensued with me and this drug dealer, and I ended up on top of him on a pool table with a pool stick in my hand, choking him until he was turning blue. The bartender called the police, and the officers broke up the fight. I don't recall if the known drug dealer was arrested or not, nor did I know whether the bar owner was cited for serving underage kids. I returned my daughter home.

Not too long after the above incident, my daughter came home with a massive black eye. Again, my daughter was in downtown Juneau, Alaska, drinking underage. I don't know how much more a father could take with the kind of behavior she was exhibiting. Obviously, I was very upset and worried about her.

I placed my Colt .45 on my hip and went looking for the man who had struck my daughter. In the downtown area, I discovered that a US Coast Guard cutter was in the harbor. There were not many military personnel in the general area that lived in Juneau year-round. I surmised that the suspect was a member of the US Coast Guard. I approached every Coast Guard officer on the street with my gun in hand and asked them if they were the one who had struck my daughter. I walked into every bar in the downtown area looking for the suspect. I had the gun in my hand as I approached each of them, and obviously, they did not tell me that they were the guilty one.

I made a drastic mistake, as I should have gone to the captain of the cutter. I was too mad to think that at the time. My daughter later told me that she would not have told me if I did see that suspect, as she thought I may have shot him. In all reality, if I would have found the suspect, I would have held him until police arrived. Again, things could have been worse, as after a few weeks or so the eye was healed.

My wife and I were at our wits' end and obviously upset and concerned about both our son and daughter. The main reason we'd left Ohio for Alaska was to have our children in a different and better environment.

CONNIE RUNS AWAY

Well, this story did not end. A month or two after the above incident, my daughter ran away from home. I had notified the state troopers that she was a runaway. I left the house to go to downtown Juneau and begin nosing around to see if anyone knew where my daughter was. I asked some kids on the street if they'd seen her, and they told me she had run away with the known drug dealer that I had encountered several months earlier.

I called my best friend Gary to meet me at the bottom of Mount Juneau with his rifle. I had learned that Connie and the drug dealer were holed up in a campground in the mountains. I notified the state troopers that I knew where my daughter was and that I was going up after her in the morning. I let them know that I was armed and a friend was going with me. They told me that they did not have an officer available to go with me in the morning; I told them that I wasn't asking for one, and that I was going after my daughter. When morning came, my friend arrived and we started up the mountain. We came upon an area with a huge waterfall and found the campground. It was early morning and it appeared that no one was awake. All was quiet except for the roar of the waterfall. I gave my friend my rifle, grabbed my .45, and began to crawl on my belly to the first tent. I searched a couple of tents until I found my daughter and this drug dealer. They were both sleeping when I entered the tent. I stuck my Colt .45 in his mouth, at which point he awoke. I made him stand up, put his pants on and walked him outside the tent. I grabbed my rifle and began to march him down the mountain side with us. As we walked down, we observed two state troopers walking up toward us. We turned the man over to the state troopers for his arrest for contributing to the delinquency of a minor and other charges that might be pending. Our job was done for the day.

THE BOAT

Not long after we arrived in Juneau, I purchased a twenty-six-foot Saber Craft, as I was told that you cannot be happy living in Juneau without having a boat. I was also told by my brother and one of his friends that I could get a sports commercial fishing license that would allow me to sell any fish that I caught. I fished mainly for halibut and salmon.

While working for Northern Sales, I sold my twenty-six-foot Saber Craft and purchased a thirty-two-foot Uniflight and obtained the sports commercial license, which allowed me to have four poles out and the ability to sell the fish that I caught.

While out fishing, I was able to observe whales, bears on the beach, eagles, and deer. Many times my friends and I would spend overnight trips while fishing for halibut. We would watch the northern lights, which were amazingly bright, as there were no city lights or other lights around, so the sky was black. The view was beautiful when the northern lights were dancing in the sky, and the dark sky allowed such a scenic view of the stars and northern lights.

One of my greatest times on that boat was when Toni's mother came to visit. Now remember, Mabel was from Ohio and had never traveled very far from home. She was absolutely amazed by the sites and new experiences she enjoyed in Juneau. She especially liked going out in the boat, which was large enough to be comfortable for an elderly woman. Once we went to Taku Harbor, a remote, small bay located on Stephan's Passage twenty-two miles southeast of Juneau. In Taku Harbor lived an old-time

Mabel and Tiger Olsen

Alaskan pioneer named Tiger Olson. Tiger was a trapper, gold miner, and a man with a colorful character. There is a public cabin there today named after him. He and Mabel became immediate friends.

MARK & PAC

I remember the day that Mark & Pac opened in Juneau. People came from all over Southeast Alaska to shop at this store, which sold items by the case. Juneau was booming because of the Trans-Alaska pipeline construction, and the residents were not used to having markets as big as Marc & Pac. Some of the people came to this store's opening, arriving from small villages. The store manager, Murray, and I got along very well from the beginning. The store was owned by a couple of Irishmen who hung out at the store quite a bit. They were both nice men, and I also got along very well with them.

NORTHERN SALES

I had been employed at the store for two years. I was working on a

Christmas display when I noticed a person watching me. The person watching me, I later discovered, was the owner of a company called Northern Sales, which was a wholesale distribution company. He seemed impressed with the display that I had arranged. He asked me if I would come to work for him as manager of his company. I told him that I would think about it and would like to see his operation. Northern Sales serviced all Southeast Alaska's drug stores, grocery stores and other small stores. They sold cigarettes, school supplies, drug store related items, and many other wholesale items. The warehouse was in downtown Juneau. I looked at the operation with Pat showing me what I would be doing. I was introduced to the other employees and Pat's wife, Connie. I accepted his offer and began working for him.

I traveled to the different Southeast communities and returned to Juneau with orders that the stores needed to have filled. I would fly to Haines, Skagway, Hoonah, Ketchikan, and other small towns in bush Alaska.

Many times the stores would call in orders for things they needed to have filled, and we would fill them and send the orders to them. While I was with Northern Sales, we acquired the opportunity to run the Pepsi and Frito Lay distributorship. While I was running Northern Sales, we set records for Pepsi and Frito Lay sales.

TONI GETS A JOB

Toni got a job in 1977 as a clerk typist for the Department of Transportation and Public Facilities. Toni worked at the Department of Transportation until 1982 and then transferred over to the State of Alaska Department of Labor as a Correspondence Secretary III.

Toni and I were driving a small orange Volkswagen for our personal transportation. One day Toni and I were driving by a local Chevrolet dealer and discovered the dealership was declaring bankruptcy and an auction was in progress. Toni wanted to stop and look at cars, so we did. Next thing you know, I was bidding on a 1979 Monte Carlo, blue in color with blue leather seats. We won the bid, paid for the vehicle and drove off in a new Monte Carlo. Toni was ecstatic. It took a while for her to get used to living in Alaska in a trailer. My daughter was working at the airport and wasn't being much trouble. Our son Bob was kept busy as a driver for Northern Sales. Bob was driving a Pepsi truck that we had acquired from the southern states, or lower 48 as it was called in Alaska. Bob worked hard at his job but was still drinking.

GRANDPARENTS

Connie eventually met Ron Brockman and started dating him. They had a child born in 1980 in Juneau, Alaska. I was able to observe the birth, and our little redhead Bobbie was born, and Toni and I became grandparents. Two years later our other granddaughter was born in 1982 on Kodiak Island where Connie and Ron now lived, and Toni was able to witness Bonnie's birth.

Toni loved to go shopping for both girls and buy them whatever they might need. They were always dressed in the best clothes money could buy. Toni's mother, Mabel, was able to visit us and really enjoyed the new boat that I had. I took her fishing whenever I could, and we explored different places in Southeast Alaska. I remember one day we were anchored at Taku Harbor, and Mabel and I went ashore. While sitting by a tree having a sandwich, something hard was pinching my bottom side from underneath the soil. It turned out to be an animal trap that I still have today.

A NEW HOME IN ALASKA

In 1978 I was able to sell the trailer that we were living in and purchase a new home near the Mendenhall Glacier. The river that flowed from the Mendenhall Glacier was our view from the backyard upper deck. The front of our house faced the mountains. My wife, Toni, was able to purchase all new furniture for our new house. I was happy that she loved her new Monte Carlo and her new home. She had earned it and deserved it. Toni loved her job and did well at it. She wore nice clothes to work and kept herself looking very nice. No one could have asked for a better companion and wife. We had been married twenty-three years, and Toni had stuck by me no matter what changes I made in my career. I was thirty-nine years old and not done changing careers.

OFFICERS KENNEDY AND ADAIR – AND ANOTHER LIFE DECISION

A terrible incident happened on April 17, 1979, in Juneau, Alaska. Officer Richard Adair and Officer Jimmy Kennedy of the Juneau Police Department were ambushed while responding to a "shots fired" call. The shooter had apparently opened fire without provocation on a neighbor and wounded him as he drove out of the driveway. The wounded driver drove down a hill, passed out and wrecked his car, prompting neighbors to call the police. As the officers pulled up near the suspect's home, he fired on both with a rifle from a second-floor window, striking them both in the head and killing them instantly. A backup officer, a responding detective, was also shot and wounded. The chief of police arrived at the scene and waited for backup from Alaska State Troopers. Before the troopers arrived, the suspect committed suicide.

Officer Adair had served with the Juneau Police Department for less than ten years. Officer Adair's son had been good friends with my son. Officer Kennedy had served with the Juneau Police Department for eighteen months.

The citizens of Juneau were saddened and shocked by the incident. The shooting occurred on Evergreen Avenue. One of the witnesses stated that during a sunny day with children at play, death came to Evergreen Avenue. Another witness stated that he had gone into the street to retrieve a beach ball as a police car passed by. The witness began to walk up the steps to the house when a series of gunshots rang out. The squad car rolled back down upper Evergreen Street with bullet holes spaced evenly about five inches apart. The car hit the power company pole behind her house and stopped. Both officers had died instantly.

Officer Adair had held his granddaughter for the first time the day before he died. Officer Kennedy had served four years in the US Navy after graduating from high school in Mississippi in 1964. Officer Kennedy was a Vietnam veteran. He moved to Juneau and was hired by the Juneau PD in 1977. The two officers' deaths affected law enforcement throughout the state of Alaska and the lower 48.

The ambush affected me profoundly, and it prompted me to spend several days thinking about my life and my intentions. I had gone through life without serving in the military, and as a small child in the orphanage, I had wanted to grow up and become a fighter pilot. Being married at sixteen and raising a family had kept me from joining the service. With all of this in mind, I decided that I would serve my country by becoming a police officer.

Officer
Richard J. Adair
Juneau Police Department, Alaska
End of Watch: Tuesday, April 17, 1979

Officer
Jimmy Earl Kennedy
Juneau Police Department, Alaska
End of Watch: Tuesday, April 17, 1979

These brave officers' deaths inspired me to become a police officer. I will never forget them.

CHAPTER SIX

JUNEAU, ALASKA, POLICE DEPARTMENT

Note from the author: This chapter will describe my time as a police officer in Juneau, Alaska. I describe my activities along with the commendations that I received. It will become clear in the next chapter why I felt it necessary that the reader have a clear understanding of what kind of officer I was, as my reputation takes an unfair beating in my next job described in Chapter 7.

I applied for a position with the Juneau Police Department. A few days after I took the test, a sergeant summoned me to the police department for a meeting. I was waiting in the lobby, sort of nervous, hoping that I would get hired. The sergeant came out to the lobby and my heart sank; *he was one of the officers that I recognized from dealing with all the problems with my children!* I said to him, "I guess I won't be getting the position."

He said, "If we had more fathers like you, we would not have any juvenile problems." I had applied for Officer Adair's job, which was a traffic position, but the sergeant told me that I would be hired as a patrolman.

Overjoyed, I rushed home to give Toni the good news. Again, she stood by me with my decision, although I think she was a little afraid. In fact, I am sure she was. Shortly after I was hired, she asked me if she could have a scanner so that she could listen to police radio calls. We bought one for her, and she would always listen in while I was on duty.

1979: TRAINING BEGINS

I was scheduled to enter the police academy in Sitka, Alaska, in October 1979. Alaska has an excellent program that I was proud to attend. In the meantime, I was issued uniforms, weapons, and a radio. I was to work with training officers for several months before going to the academy in Sitka. I was deeply proud that I was now a police officer serving the city of Juneau, Alaska. The capitol city.

One evening I was driving the patrol car with my training officer, JP, a former special forces soldier who had served in Vietnam. As I turned the patrol car ninety degrees to make a left turn, he suddenly cracked me in the chest and yelled out, "You failed to look at the rooftops when you turned the corner!"

I enjoyed having JP as my training officer. He was a solid guy and a member of my karate group. I worked with him until my assignment at the Sitka Police Academy.

Late in 1979, I was sent to the Public Safety Academy's Sixteenth Municipal Police Academy in Sitka, Alaska. The training would last approximately six weeks. During my time there, we were kept continuously busy with both physical fitness and classroom activities. I was the oldest officer in the class at thirty-nine years old but was in excellent physical condition.

During our physical fitness training, at one session, the state trooper in charge asked me to lead physical fitness exercises. We would start off with eight-count pushups. With the trooper by my side, we started doing the eight-count pushups. I don't recall the number of eight-count pushups we were doing, but the trooper in charge looked over at me while we were performing them. His face was very red, and he was in dire need of stopping.

He said to me, "You son of a gun. I will never let you lead calisthenics again!"

I continued the eight-count pushups while several of the students could no longer do them.

During my time at the police academy, the class was summoned to assist the City and Bureau of Sitka, Alaska's, police department. We were to assist them in a search for a lost hunter in the high mountainous Green Lake area, southeast of Sitka. The search was a night search and in dangerous terrain. The body of the hunter was recovered early the next morning, making the search a success. Each of our class received a thank you letter from the chief of police.

Another incident that occurred while I was there was a fire that had started near the city wharf. The wind was blowing from the water area to the west, causing the fire to spread. Again, our police academy personnel were summoned to help. When we arrived on site, the fire was nearing a gun store. The trooper in charge asked me to guard a school bus that was being loaded with weapons and ammunition from the gun shop. The trooper told me to grab a shotgun and appoint someone else to assist. The academy personnel loaded the entire inventory from the gun shop to an old school bus. The evening was a success, and the fire was extinguished.

GRADUATION AND NEW LIFE
AS OFFICER KARL

At the graduation award ceremony, our squad, which was called C squad, conducted or did the most pushups during the academy. Each of us was awarded a plaque. I won first place in the Municipal Police Academy precision driving award. I did not realize there was a contest but was proud to accept the first-place award. We all graduated except for one person. We were given the oath of office given by an FBI agent; it was one of several of the proudest moments of my life.

I returned to Juneau, Alaska, to begin my new career in law enforcement. The Juneau PD ID card was given to me, along with the other ID that was a commission as an Alaska State Trooper. I would be assigned a training officer to help me adapt to a full-time patrolman. I would work with the training officer for six or eight weeks.

I was now assigned to my own vehicle and given a shift. I was able to get acquainted with the other officers in the department and the rest of the staff, including the chief. The current chief would be retiring or leaving the department very soon, so I didn't really get to know him that well.

POST-GRADUATION; GENERAL SITUATION IN JUNEAU

Juneau, Alaska, was a tourist attraction, and at times there were two or three large cruise ships anchored in the channel. I enjoyed my duties, especially during the time when many tourists were in town. I would exit my patrol car and walk the downtown area, as the department was requested to do. As a rookie cop, I had purchased a bullet-resistant Kevlar groin protector in case I was ever shot in the privates! You never know, right? Well, when it arrived in the mail, I put it on over my private parts before leaving home. I was proudly walking foot patrol in downtown Juneau smiling at the tourists when I felt my "protector" sliding down my pant leg. The damn thing was protecting my ankle when I bent over to pick it up. Several persons saw what I was doing, and this started my uncontrollable laugh. I did not tell them what it was but sheepishly walked away still laughing. I got back to the police department where everyone had a good laugh, especially the dispatch ladies.

Alcohol was a problem downtown, and we were required to do many bar checks. When we were off duty and the cruise ships were in, we were able to board the ships and mingle with the passengers. Many times military ships would be in the harbor, both Canadian and US.

One day I was walking the streets during day shift when I observed a white male slumped over the steering wheel of a vehicle. I approached the vehicle, knocked on the window several times and finally got the person's attention. The individual slid over to the passenger side of the vehicle, exited and was walking away from me. I asked him to stop, as I needed to talk to him. He continued walking away when he abruptly turned and came toward me in a threatening manner and stated that he was going to come "right through me." I hit him with my fist, and he fell to the ground. He was a large fellow, heavily built, but he went down, and I handcuffed and arrested him for disorderly conduct and public drunkenness. I later found out that the other officers knew him, and that he was associated with drug activity.

On December 21, I was at the station having a cup of coffee when I was told by dispatch that one of the officers was not answering his radio. I left the station and found the officer's vehicle parked near the ferry terminal. After I had left the station, a call had come in that the hotel had been robbed, and the lady at the desk had been sexually assaulted. The hotel was near the police station. I saw that my partner was not in his vehicle. I parked my vehicle and was getting out when I heard two gunshots. The shots were coming from a covered stairway leading up to an apartment. I pulled my weapon and started up the stairway. When I arrived at the top, I found my partner standing there. He was okay, so I turned and broke down the door to the apartment. We both went inside where we observed about half a dozen Alaska natives in the apartment. Sitting in a chair was a large male holding a large ring of keys, which we assumed were from the hotel. The subject was arrested and taken to the station and placed in a holding cell wearing just a shirt and shorts. My partner asked dispatch to call in detectives, as it was after hours.

The detective sergeants arrived quickly and, while walking toward me in the station hallway, one of them said, "Who do you have hanging in the cell?"

I rushed back to the cell and saw that the prisoner had hanged himself using his shirt. The medics were called, but even though they were close by and responded immediately, they could not revive him.

Now other officers were called in to help with the investigation.

I was asked to go back to the scene to see where the bullet holes were in the covered stairway. I did as I was told and searched the stairway but could not find any bullet holes. I returned to the station, not knowing why shots were fired or how many. I was then told by my partner that he had followed the footprints in the fresh snow from the hotel to the apartment building leading up the stairway. He had drawn his revolver, and while walking up the stairway to the apartment, he slipped, and his handgun went off. Because the shots were fired in a covered stairway, when I thought I heard two shots, it must have been an echo that I thought was a second shot.

On one occasion I responded to a call of a trespasser at a local motel. I was the only officer available to respond when I arrived at the motel. The trespassing incident occurred on the second floor. I climbed the stairs and entered a room where the trespasser was located. Things did not go too well, as the young suspect and I got involved in an altercation. The suspect was very strong, and we were wrestling on the floor of the small landing outside the sliding doors. We ended up on the outside small patio.

As the struggle continued, the suspect and I managed to both be on our feet, and I saw him reaching into his back pocket. I drew my revolver as he was approaching me in a threatening manner and began to squeeze the trigger. In a matter of a second or so, his brother came out of the room and assisted me in the arrest. This all happened very quickly, as I was already on the first click of my revolver. The next squeeze would have been a chest shot.

Later in the week we received a letter from the motel owners stating as follows:

"We would like to take this opportunity to express our gratitude and appreciation to officer LEWKOWSKI for his performance to duty when he responded to a call for assistance from our establishment at 3 AM, 3 September, 1980. He was thrust into a situation where not only was property damage imminent, but a direct danger to the officer's life was evident due to the circumstances of the situation.

What could have become a tragic event was averted by the professionalism and calm manner in which the officer conducted himself and when force was needed to carry out the assignment only the amount required was used. Thank you again for your response and we feel the department can only be credited by your actions and professional manner."

Signed: Jim and MPS Henry

DRIFTWOOD LODGE
435 WILLOUGHBY AVENUE
JUNEAU, ALASKA 99801
(907) 586-2280

3 September 1980
Juneau, Alaska

To: Chief of Police, Juneau, Alaska
    Officer Lewkowski
Subj: letter of appreciation

We would like to take this opportunity to express our gratitude and appreciation to officer LEWKOWSKI for his performance to duty when he responded to a call for assistance from our establishment at 3am 3 September 1980.
He was thrust into a situation where not only was property damage imminent, but a direct danger to the officers life was evident due to the circumstances of the situation.
What could have become a tragic event was averted by the professionalism and calm manner in which the officer conducted himself and when force was needed to carry out the assignment only the amount required was used.
Thank you again for your response and we feel the department can only be credited by your actions and professional manner.

DEPARTMENT OF POLICE
R E C E I V E D
1980
Juneau, Alaska

Jim and Peggy Henry
DRIFTWOOD LODGE

On September 18, 1980, Juneau Police Department Capt. Joseph Ciraulo was named chief of police. I respected Chief Ciraulo very much during the time he was chief.

The chief was a very neat person and took pride in the way the department was kept clean. Sometimes when he arrived, there would be four to five street people in the lobby who might not have smelled particularly good. The chief would call us into the office and ask us what was going on. We told him that we would have to remarry the couples out in the lobby (more on this later). He looked at us quite sternly, and we left his office.

HOME LIFE

Everything seemed to be going well at home; Toni had her new car, and we had a new home that was nicely furnished. Toni had also started working for the State of Alaska Department of Transportation and Public Facilities as a Clerk Typist III. She managed the entire office: filing, routing all phone calls, making travel arrangements, collecting mail and ordering supplies. She worked there until 1982, in April, when she began working for the State of Alaska Department of Labor as a Correspondence Secretary III; she worked there until February 1984.

Toni and I also enjoyed our new thirty-two-foot Uniflite. Toni would accompany me on fishing trips when the weather was good. Bob was working at Mark & Pac as a meat cutter and reported for work every day. He eventually left Mark & Pac to begin working at Northern Sales when I was manager.

My son went through a bad phase with alcohol and had to do some time in the Lemon Creek Correctional Center in Juneau. On his first day in prison, Bob was lined up for the evening meal when a large black man beckoned him over to his table and asked him to sit down. The man asked my son if Corporal Lewk was his father. My son replied that he was wondering if this was going to be a good thing or a bad thing. The man said that your dad treated him fairly during his arrest. He also said that your dad could have roughed me up but instead treated me with as much dignity as he could under the circumstances. No one will mess with you while you are in here, he told Bob.

Another incident occurred when my son attended an AA meeting. An Alaska native was speaking to the group and asked if anyone had any contact with Corporal Lewk. Several people raised their hands. The speaker stated that Corporal Lewk was "the fairest cop we have had in Juneau, but don't mess with him."

In those days I was studying karate with Sensei Tanaka, based out of Anchorage, Alaska. Sensei Tanaka has gained international recognition for his contribution to this sport. Karl Stewart was the instructor in Juneau, Alaska, whom I studied under. I received a diploma from the Kenwa Karate Association, earning a third-degree green belt rating in that group. I also competed in the Alaska Police Olympics in Anchorage, Alaska, where I won three silver medals and six bronze medals during that period.

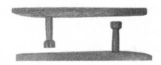

Tonfa sticks

While with JPD, I was awarded instructor certification to teach PR-24, which, in karate, is called a Tonfa. A Tonfa is an ancient Okinawan farming tool that peasants adapted for use as a defense against sword attacks. It consists of a stick with a perpendicular handle a third of the way down the length of the stick. The Tonfa is a formidable weapon but still no match for a .45 ACP.

My partner and I were often called to domestic disturbances on the night shift. My partner reminded me of the actor John Candy. John came up with our strategy for nonviolent domestic disturbances. We would "divorce" the couples for the evening. If they behaved, stayed apart overnight, and reported to the station in the morning, we would remarry them. This tactic seemed to work many times, and we would not have to arrest anyone when there was no violence to report. Obviously if one party were injured, one would go to jail. It was our way of establishing the peace for the evening.

My partner also came up with a strategy for the youngsters we would encounter on the streets. We would gather the young kids who were out at night and make them raise their right hands and swear to report any illegal activity to us. They did, and it was in good humor. The kids kind of enjoyed it, as they thought they were deputies.

I worked with a great bunch of guys and enjoyed working with them on different shifts. We had our differences, but we got along. Several of our JPD officers resigned to take positions with the Alaska State Troopers.

It was interesting to note the bars in Juneau, Alaska, at the time I was a police officer, could remain open until five am. On May 31, 1984, the assembly adopted an ordinance requiring bars to close at two am every day of the week. This was a good thing, for alcohol in Juneau caused many of the problems in our community.

I recall one incident, among many, when I encountered a female in the park near the police station. It was dark when I met the young lady in the park, and she began talking to me. I had a tape recorder in my shirt pocket, so I began to tape the stories that she was telling me. I don't know why she opened to me so quickly, but she began to tell me about her experiences working as an undercover person for the federal government. I must have recorded at least an hour, maybe more, of conversation relating to her undercover work that, if I remember correctly, she was still involved with. I couldn't believe that she started talking to me about the work that she was doing. What she told me was quite dangerous and was related to gangs on the West Coast: narcotics, beatings, and illegal activities by biker gangs. At one point, I knew my tape recorder was running low and was ready to quit. I told the lady that I had to urinate and that I would be right back. I changed the tape and began another tape recording of the conversation.

After my shift was over, I gave the tapes to our Sgt. Detective and advised him of the content of the tape. He, in turn, turned the tapes over to our local FBI agent, who was quite shocked that this female would talk to me that long about the work she was doing for the feds.

SERT RESPONSE TEAM

In August of 1981, eight other officers and I were assigned to the newly formed Special Emergency Response Team, or SERT, and issued our equipment. Our team was on a training mission on February 11, 1980. During the training exercise, we used our department-issued Smith & Wesson .357 revolvers instead of the Colt .45s that were on order. The officer in charge advised all team members to clean their weapons before reporting for duty. I had been around guns since I had been thirteen or fourteen years of age and knew how to handle weapons safely. I took my revolver home and removed it from my holster, which was a clam shell-type holster. The revolver was unloaded, and I began to clean the revolver at my kitchen table. I finished cleaning the revolver and walked to my upstairs bedroom to where my Sam Browne belt was lying on the bed in my spare bedroom. I loaded the weapon and placed it back into the clam shell holster.

As I was leaving the bedroom, I glanced back at the revolver lying on the bed and saw that the hammer was cocked. As I walked toward the bed, I had my finger extended to keep it from striking. I was several inches away, never touching the trigger because I had intended to place my finger in front of the hammer so it would not strike the firing pin. The firearm discharged and the bullet struck my left leg below the knee. I believe the vibration from my wooden floors may have caused the hammer to fall forward, causing the weapon to fire. As I understand it, with the Smith & Wesson Model 19, to fire the weapon one would have to pull the trigger. It is obvious from looking at the holster that the trigger was covered, and I could not have pulled the trigger. I lay on the floor bleeding profusely from my leg. My wife was screaming as I was telling her to call 911.

When the squad arrived, there was quite a bit of blood on my carpet. The crew transported me to the hospital where I underwent surgery to remove fragments of the .357 bullet from my leg. On the way to the hospital, I was more concerned about the blood on my living room floor carpet then I was with my injury, but lo and behold, I later found out my little dog Lady had cleaned the carpet such that no one could tell there was blood on it. Man's best friend took care of things. I always wondered what it would be like to be shot, and now I knew. It's as if my leg went into shock because it was shaking so bad that I really don't remember feeling the pain. They did a remarkable job on the surgery, and after I recovered, I was able to continue my exercise routine, running and jogging. I later learned that the firearm had a safety bar so that one could not fire the weapon unless the trigger was physically squeezed. I did not pull the trigger, as the trigger was covered by the holster. I believe I was off work for approximately eleven days.

We soon received our new weapon, a Colt .45 semi-automatic handgun for our duty weapon. I was very thankful for that.

I was the first officer to carry a Colt .45 on duty in uniform; the weapon was carried, cocked, and locked. I carried the weapon for the first time for two weeks. I received one comment from an Alaska native when he stated to me, "Officer, do you know your weapon is cocked?" I advised him that I was carrying it the correct way. This was the only comment that I recall during the two weeks I carried the forty-five caliber Colt.

My fellow officers gave me a safety award-a plaque with my damaged holster mounted!

I was giving the briefing to the day shift one morning, and I had my new colt .45 on my hip with a thirty-round magazine inserted. The chief walked into my briefing room and stared at my hip, then walked away from me. When the briefing was over, he called me on the PA system. "Corporal Luke, report to my office!" He looked very sternly at me and said, "What do you have on your weapon?"

I said, "I AM NOT RUNNING OUT OF AMMO AS THE GUYS DID IN OUR LATEST SHOOT OUT!"

He gave me the weirdest of looks as I was leaving his office.

Being a member of our newly formed SERT team, we all received many hours of training. I was sent to the Smith & Wesson Academy in Springfield, Massachusetts, where I was the designated gas person for the team. That means I was trained and responsible for using the tear gas in the event an emergency called for it. While at this training, I learned that there would be a special shotgun training class following it. I called back to the chief to see if he would authorize me to stay and attend the shotgun class, as we did not have anyone on the force who had taken it. He approved this additional training, as our biggest expense was travel and I was already here.

I didn't mention this, but an additional benefit was that my wife had accompanied me on this trip. She had a great time, even getting to visit Hyannis Port and see the Kennedy Compound.

Also, I was sent to Fort Lewis, Washington, for training, where I received special SWAT team training. I believe this training took a week with an FBI instructor.

PROMOTION TO CORPORAL

I was promoted to Corporal of Police in September 1981, a position I held until I left the department in 1986. During that time, I received a commendation for meritorious service in 1983, a letter of commendation in April 1985, and a letter of commendation in August 1985.

One evening, in April 1982, I was acting as a training officer. I had a new officer with me, and we were working together in the patrol car. I observed a male subject, known by all the officers, walking around South Franklin St. carrying a blue backpack. I advised the officer with me to write an FI (field interview) card on the subject, noting the time and date that we observed him, as well as his clothing description. The FI cards were kept in a file at the police station. Some officers felt that these cards were a waste of time.

DOUBLE HOMICIDE

Approximately ten days later, two bodies were found in an apartment close by the police department. Both the male and female deceased were brutally murdered and sexually assaulted. The coroner ruled that they had been deceased for approximately nine days. Prior to this event, we had filled out those field interview cards. The importance of the cards was never questioned after this.

Juneau Police Field Interview Card

We began a search for the suspect for whom we had filled out the FI card. He was arrested a short time later by detectives and was charged with the murders. Forensic evidence—a print and a hair sample—were found at the scene. I testified at the trial as to the field interview cards we filed that morning. That placed the suspect in the vicinity at the time of the crime. The suspect was sentenced to ninety-nine years in prison. Another subject was a suspect but was not charged for the crime.

Just an interesting note regarding the double homicide. The second suspect who was acquitted in that murder of the couple in the Franklin Street apartment in 1982 was gunned down by a man who told Juneau Police Officers that was something that he just had to do. The other subject that I spoke of was already serving a ninety-nine-year sentence for the crime. The person gunned down was thought to be his partner.

1982 SUPREME COURT CASE

Another case that I recall was a DUI arrest that I made in May of 1982, where I used my tape recorder as soon as I recognized a possible DUI suspect. The bottom line on this matter was that the defendant tried to suppress the tape recording. Eventually it wound up in the Alaska Supreme Court, which ruled in favor of the tape recording that I had made of the suspect. The case was filed under the name of Quinto vs. the City and Borough of Juneau, Alaska. The case set an important legal precedent regarding the use of tape recordings as a legal tactic.

664 P.2d 630 (1983)
Marcelo QUINTO, Jr., Appellant,

v.

CITY AND BOROUGH OF JUNEAU, Appellee.

No. 7334.

Court of Appeals of Alaska.

June 17, 1983.

Early in the morning of May 31, 1982, Marcelo Quinto, Jr., was arrested for driving a motor vehicle while under the influence of intoxicants (DWI) in violation of City and Borough of Juneau Municipal Code § 72.10.010.

Quinto was observed driving his Ford Bronco erratically near Whittier Street in downtown Juneau by a Juneau police officer, who communicated Quinto's location, license plate number, and make of car to another officer, Corporal Karl Lewkowski. Lewkowski drove to the area and saw a "Bronco-type vehicle" with its brake lights on at the top of a ramp leading to the Prospector Hotel; no other vehicles were in sight.

Lewkowski drove up the ramp and verified the license plate number on the Bronco. He then approached Quinto, who was behind the wheel; as he walked toward the Bronco, Lewkowski activated a small tape recorder that was attached to his belt. When he got to the Bronco, Lewkowski noticed that Quinto had bloodshot eyes and smelled of alcohol. Lewkowski concluded that Quinto was intoxicated and asked him to perform field sobriety tests. After performing poorly on the sobriety tests, Quinto was arrested. All pre-arrest communications between Lewkowski and Quinto were recorded without Quinto's knowledge on Lewkowski's tape recorder. Quinto later repeated the sobriety tests on videotape at the Juneau Police Department, but he refused to submit to a breathalyzer examination.

On appeal, Quinto asserts that the trial court committed error by refusing to allow expert testimony concerning Quinto's blood alcohol level at the time of his arrest by excluding testimony concerning Quinto's reputation for sobriety in the community, and by denying a motion to suppress the tape recording that was made without Quinto's permission prior to his arrest. We reverse.

FEMALE ESCAPEE

One day in 1983, the US Marshal's Office informed us that a female subject, now in Juneau, was at large and considered armed and extremely dangerous. She had escaped confinement three times and had attempted escape eight times. She had escaped from Michigan State Corrections in 1982 while serving two life sentences for two counts of first-degree murder, plus eight to ten years for attempted murder. She was believed to be aided in her escape by a male subject who was employed at the prison.

The US Marshal in Juneau advised me that the subject was in our city. We planned an all-night stakeout of her apartment that our investigation uncovered. During our investigation, we discovered that the apartment the suspect was in was scheduled to be visited by a plumber in the morning to fix a leak. The US Marshal and I drove an old pickup truck dressed as plumbers and carried a toolbox. We knocked at the door, and the suspect answered. We placed her under arrest and handcuffed her without incident. Also standing by was the eight-member emergency response team who were to assist in her apprehension if needed. Also arrested was the prison vocational instructor who helped her to escape and was traveling with her.

MANHUNT

In 1983, an individual had escaped from the Lemon Creek Correctional Center in Juneau, Alaska. Our department and the Alaska State Troopers in the city were conducting a manhunt for this individual. A friend of my son's girlfriend had knowledge of where the suspect, the escapee, was staying and could currently be located. I passed the information on to my Sgt., and we prepared a plan where I would go in with the female to her friend's apartment where the suspect was located. The entire team was utilized in the effort that proved successful, as the suspect was in the house. If I recall, he was quite wet and cold from being up the mountainside for a long period before he hid out in this apartment. Backup arrived and entered quickly behind me. It was another coordinated team effort.

The letter from the Chief of Police states:

Corporal Lewkowski,

Please be advised that it is a privilege and an honor to present to you this Commendation for Meritorious Service for the action you took on the evening of March 9, 1983, in recapturing an escaped felon.

THE CITY AND BOROUGH OF JUNEAU
CAPITAL OF ALASKA
155 SOUTH SEWARD ST.   JUNEAU, ALASKA 99801

March 15, 1983

Corporal Karl R. Lewkowski
4531 Riverside Drive
Juneau, Alaska 99801

Subject: Commendation for Meritorious Service:

Dear Corporal Lewkowski:

Please be advised that it is a privilege and an honor to present to you this Commendation for Meritorious Service for the action you took on the evening of March 9, 1983, in recapturing an escaped felon.

On that date, Roy C. Marshall, a 35 year old inmate serving 10 years for armed robbery, who escaped from the Southeast Correctional Center at Lemon Creek, a maximum security facility, had reportedly taken refuge in an apartment in West Juneau.

Posing as a friend of a woman living at the apartment, who informed on the subject, you and she entered the residence and you immediately "got the drop" on him before he could react.

Marshall, reported to be a dangerous man, was surprised and surrendered without incident.

Even though your entry and subsequent action of subduing the subject was immediately followed by other members of our department and state troopers, your unselfish and courageous deed resulted in the quick and safe apprehension of a dangerous felon with minimal risk to law enforcement officers and others involved.

Please accept my sincere congratulations on a difficult and stressful task well done.

Sincerely,

Joseph R. Ciraulo
Chief of Police

Copied from Karl's records

On that date, Roy C. Marshall, a thirty-five-year-old inmate serving ten years for armed robbery, who escaped from the Southeast Correctional Center at Lemon Creek, a maximum-security facility, had reportedly taken refuge in an apartment in West Juneau.

Posing as a friend of a woman living in the apartment, who informed on the subject, you and she entered the residence and you immediately "got the drop" on him before he could react. Marshall, reported to be a dangerous man, was surprised and surrendered without incident.

Even though your entrance and subsequent action of subduing the subject was immediately followed by other members of our department and state troopers, your unselfish and courageous deed resulted in the quick and safe apprehension of a dangerous felon with minimal risk to law enforcement officers and others involved.

Please accept my sincere congratulations on a difficult and stressful task well done.

Signed: Joseph R. Ciraulo, Chief of Police

NEW CHIEF AND A COMMENDATION

In July of 1985, Chief Ciraulo retired and Capt. Michael Gelston replaced him as chief. I will never forget the time Chief Ciraulo called me to his office and sat me down. He asked me not to tell anyone in the department what he was going to tell me. I said that I would not tell anyone. I was never more proud and held this inside of me for many years, but the chief told me that I was the best street cop that he had ever worked with or words somehow to that effect. I never told anyone in the department. I was so proud of what he told me.

On August 6, 1985, my sergeant requested that I receive a letter of commendation regarding an arrest at the ferry terminal. In his conversation with the chief and later in a report, he described the incident as follows:

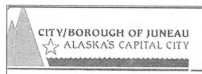

CITY/BOROUGH OF JUNEAU
☆ ALASKA'S CAPITAL CITY

LETTER OF COMMENDATION

August 15, 1985

Corporal Karl R. Lewkowski

Dear Corporal Lewkowski:

Due to your actions on July 15, 1985, resulting in the arrest of William and Audrey Lawrence, I would like to take this opportunity to recognize those efforts.

Your handling of the matter was undertaken and accomplished in the truest sense of a professional law enforcement officer. The situation involved confrontation with an extremely intractable couple; a confrontation you handled in a poised and professional manner in front of a large gathering of people at the Ferry Terminal. Your handling of the incident resulted in many favorable comments as to the disposition of the situation.

During this incident you exhibited and displayed many of the traits for which we involved in law enforcement strive. As a result, you greatly enhanced the image of the Juneau Police Department in the eyes of the community. Efforts such as yours garner large rewards for the Police Department in respect to civilian perception of our efforts as well as acknowledgement of our expertise. Once again, I wish to extend to you my sincere thanks for your truly professional efforts and hold up those efforts as an example for others to follow.

Sincerely,

Michael S. Gelston
Chief of Police

Copied from Karl's records

"A subject was at the ferry terminal ranting and raving and was very uncooperative. He was cursing at Cpl. Lewkowski, saying things like, F you asshole! This was repeated numerous times. The suspect would get right up next to Cpl. Lewkowski's face as he was yelling and cursing. Lawrence was being abusive toward Cpl. Lewkowski as he was throwing his license and registration at the Cpl. and being quite obnoxious. When Lawrence was making threatening gestures toward Cpl. Lewkowski, Lawrence would clench his fist and make movements toward Cpl. Lewkowski, knowing that an arrest was imminent. Lewkowski radioed for backup before proceeding to make the physical arrest. Knowing that William Lawrence was an ex-professional boxer, Lewkowski knew that he would most likely have to hurt him if he attempted the arrest by himself. There were at least two hundred people in the immediate vicinity while this was taking place. Most of them were tourists. Cpl. Lewkowski swallowed his pride and maintained his cool in the face of this adversity, as numerous witnesses stated they felt Cpl. Lewkowski did an exceptionally fine job regarding the arrest. They say that he acted with an extreme amount of restraint in dealing with the suspect. At no time did any witness observe the Cpl. demonstrate any behavior or mannerisms that could be construed as aggressive. They, in fact, stated that Cpl. acted in a very nonviolent and professional manner. Some witnesses went as far as to say after the arrest was affected that it must be rewarding to work with someone like that."

The Chief of Police then wrote the following commendation letter:

Dear Corpora, Lewkowski:

Due to your actions on July 15, 1985, resulting in the arrest of William and Audrey Lawrence, I would like to take this opportunity to recognize those efforts.

Your handling of the matter was undertaken and accomplished in the truest sense of a professional law enforcement officer. The situation involved confrontation with an extremely intractable couple; a confrontation you handled in a poised and professional manner in front of a large gathering of people at the ferry terminal. Your handling of the incident resulted in many favorable comments as to the disposition of the situation.

During this incident you exhibited and displayed many of the traits for which we involved in law enforcement strive. As a result, you greatly enhanced the image of the Juneau Police Department in the eyes of the community. Efforts such as yours garner large rewards for the Police Department in respect to civilian perception of our efforts as well as acknowledgement of our expertise. Once again, I wish to extend my sincere thanks for your truly professional efforts and hold up those efforts as an example for others to follow.

Signed: Michael S. Gelston, Chief of Police.

OFFICER SUICIDE

The officer that was with me on the double homicide case in 1982 died of a self-inflicted gunshot in March 1986. His death was one of the saddest moments in my police career. He was loved by many people in our community and was a great hit with many of the young kids.

In January 1986, officer Bill Ireland was named the new Youth Officer for the Juneau School District and Juneau Police Department Cooperative Youth Crime Prevention and Education Program. Officer Ireland was a four-year veteran. On March 7, 1986, Officer Bill Ireland died from a self-inflicted gunshot wound. He was loved by all.

Police officers are at a higher risk of suicide than any other profession. In fact, suicide is so prevalent in the profession that in a recent study it was found that the number of police officers who died by suicide is more than triple that of police officers killed in the line of duty. The things they see and the stress involved on the job are major causes of this horrible statistic.

GENERAL INCIDENTS AND MEMORIES FROM JPD

Most of the time I spent with JPD was on swing-shift and graveyard-shift. At one point, I recall being scheduled for dayshift. While patrolling the area by the local schools, I started using the radar gun. To my astonishment, I was getting readings of anywhere from 25 to 55, and even 60 miles per hour in the school zones. I remember school zone violations being mandatory court appearances and six points on your driver's license. I once received a phone call from the local judge who said to me words to the effect of, "What are you doing to my courtroom? It is standing room only." I explained to the judge that, of all tickets written, most of them were in direct violation of the 25 miles an hour speed limit or 20 miles per hour speed limit. Some tickets were 25 to 30 miles per hour over the speed limit. The dispatchers also told me that they have never heard so much radio traffic on day shift. I was on a mission to protect the kids near the schools.

I recall another incident during the winter months and, perhaps, during Christmas time when I was walking foot patrol in the downtown area. I normally would walk on foot during the cold weather, as sometimes I would find intoxicated persons coddled up under a stairway. I remember checking an abandoned building where I noticed a stove with the door off and the stove was working, providing minimal heat. While walking toward the stove, I noticed several male subjects sleeping near the stove area. Upon further inspection, I noticed a small boy cuddled up near the stove with minimal clothing. I carefully picked the boy up and headed to my patrol car. I contacted the family service agency and told them that I would be bringing the boy to their location, as I feared for his welfare and the unsafe conditions of the abandoned building. I also notified another social agency to check on the condition of the male subjects that were sleeping in the building.

Thinking about my time with JPD, I recall how easy it was for people on the street to talk to me, as I walked foot patrol quite often on my shifts. I was practicing community policing before the college professors even came up with the term.

It required dedication to be a member of a SWAT team or a narcotics team; it always involved major teamwork among the investigators and informants. One case may take hundreds of hours of surveillance to culminate a major drug arrest and conviction during the time I was assigned to the drug unit in Alaska. We used confidential informants to infiltrate liquor establishments and root out drug sellers. Our hours were flexible as required and rank was not important. We worked as a team. Safety was our first concern for officers and informants. We escalated our buys to convict the major suppliers in the city utilizing other police departments, including the patrolmen on the streets, for information.

Undercover informants were given enough money to complete their buys and to perform their mission. I enjoyed the work immensely and was personally satisfied. The work we did made me a better investigator and police officer. At one time our unit was advised by the DA's office to lay off for a while, as we were flooding their office with a heavy caseload. The DA were dedicated professionals, efficient and hard-working individuals. I enjoyed my role as a narcotics investigator, gaining experience in search warrants, raids, affidavits and surveillance procedures. Surveillance makes drug cases! In later years, this training proved invaluable in my future role as a private investigator.

Since I was a corporal, I would occasionally be selected for "other duties" requiring management and organizational ability. Such was my participation in organizing the department's annual Law Enforcement Day Memorial Ceremony, as explained in the following letter:

CITY/BOROUGH OF JUNEAU
☆ **ALASKA'S CAPITAL CITY**

April 19, 1985

Corporal Karl R. Lewkowski
4531 Riverside Drive
Juneau, Alaska 99801

Subject: <u>Letter of Commendation:</u>

Dear Corporal Lewkowski:

On behalf of the Juneau Police Department and the other police and military agencies represented, I wish to commend you for the time and energy devoted to the Seventh Annual Law Enforcement Day Memorial Ceremony held April 17, 1985.

Without much advance notice and experience in this kind of project, you did a very fine job of planning, organizing and coordinating the service.

Your idea of calling upon the military, such as the U. S. Coast Guard and Army National Guard to provide members for an honor guard and rifle team to fire a 21 gun salute in addition to seeking out a citizen to play <u>Amazing Grace</u> on the bagpipes, was impressive and most appreciated.

Such action showed imagination and creative thinking on your part. And it strengthened our community relations and the department's inter-agency cooperation with the military. For this I thank you.

Sincerely,

Joseph R. Ciraulo
Chief of Police
Juneau Police Department
210 Admiral Way

JRC/plh

Copied from Karl's records

On behalf of the Juneau Police Department and the other police and military agencies represented, I wish to commend you for the time and energy devoted to the Seventh Annual Law Enforcement Day Memorial Ceremony held April 17, 1985.

Without much advance notice and experience in this kind of project, you did a very fine job of planning, organizing and coordinating the service.

Your idea of calling upon the military, such as the U.S. Coast Guard and Army National Guard, to provide members for an honor guard and rifle team to fire a 21 gun salute in addition to seeking out a citizen to play Amazing Grace on the bagpipes, was impressive and most appreciated.

Such action showed imagination and creative thinking on your part. And it strengthened our community relations and the department's inter-agency cooperation with the military. For this I thank you.

Signed by Joseph R. Ciraulo, Chief of Police.

DRUGS

My last assignment with JPD was with the State Metro Drug Unit, where an Alaska State Trooper sergeant was in charge. I was extremely fortunate to be assigned to this unit where we worked as a team on all drug purchases, surveillance, etc. At times, we conducted surveillance in other Southeast Alaska communities when requested by their city officials. The experience I received working with this special group was to be invaluable to my decision to pursue another career when I returned to Ohio. The Sgt. of the unit also gave me the assignment of being control officer for one of our confidential informants. While with the narcotics unit, the confidential informant I'm speaking of generated a total of twenty or so cases while I was his control officer.

I conducted a surveillance one evening where our confidential informant purchased drugs and was in the vehicle with the seller. The informant was wired up, and, while following their vehicle, I heard them comment that there was a cop following him. I was the surveillance officer in another vehicle. When I heard this comment, I didn't react at first, but when the seller yelled out again, "I know that's a cop following us!" I put my foot down on the gas pedal and passed them at high speed. As I passed them and returned to the lane of traffic in front of them, I began weaving side to side. I heard the driver and the seller of the drugs yell out, "He is not a cop, he's drunker than hell!" while my other team member took over my surveillance position. We followed our seller to his destination. While working with the Metro Drug Unit, we conducted major cases involving dealers, and we always pursued a higher level of drug activity. It was an honor working with the professionals I worked with in the Metro Drug Unit.

During my tenure with JPD, I received numerous training hours and classes—too many to mention. The training I received was instrumental in my pursuit of a new career when I arrived in Ohio.

CLOSING THOUGHTS

I had moved to Juneau, Alaska, hoping to find work in the grocery industry. I was leaving as a highly-trained police officer. My two kids were now grown and supporting themselves. I left with many regrets but looked forward to returning home to see where my newly acquired skills would take me.

I was proud of my "street creds" and recall several incidents that validate my feelings that my reputation among the street people of Juneau was of a fair and honest cop.

Leaving Alaska was difficult for me as I loved the place! [photo credit]

I close out this chapter with a letter of recommendation I received from Sgt. Kalwara. I submit this to my readers to bear in mind as they read what happens to me in my next job.

It is with regret that we would lose an officer such as Corporal Lewkowski. Since, however, he has chosen to leave our department, I feel compelled to write a letter of recommendation. I have worked with Corporal Lewkowski for the past seven (7) years.

I have always found him to be hardworking and dedicated. When given an assignment, he works diligently, completes it promptly and follows instructions. Corporal Lewkowski is a "team player" and has always put the department ahead of his own personal gain. I could go on, but I think it would suffice to say that Corporal Lewkowski always carries himself in a very professional manner.

During his tenure with the Juneau Police Department, Corporal Lewkowski has attended numerous training classes and seminars; too numerous to mention here. He has worked hard in these classes and represented the department well. We have kept records of our training; a copy of which Corporal Lewkowski has sent to you. I can attest to the fact that Corporal Lewkowski has in fact attended all training listed. For further verification, a training record is also kept and certified with the Alaska Police Standards Council."

DEPARTMENT OF PUBLIC SAFETY
DIVISION OF STATE TROOPERS

TO: ~~████ ██ ████~~
FROM: Sergeant Kalwara
DATE: 5-20-86
RE: Corporal Lewkowski

It is with regret that we would lose an Officer such as Corporal Lewkowski. Since, however, he has chosen to leave our department, I feel compelled to write a letter of recommendation.

I have worked with Corporal Lewkowski for the past seven (7) years. I have always found him to be hardworking and dedicated. When given an assignment, he works diligently, completes it promptly and follows instructions. Corporal Lewkowski is a "team player", and has always put the department ahead of his own personal gain. I could go on, but I think it would suffice to say that Corporal Lewkowski always carries himself in a very professional manner.

During his tenure with the Juneau Police Department, Corporal Lewkowski has attended numerous training classes and seminars; too numerous to mention here. He has worked hard in these classes and represented the department well. We have kept records of our training; a copy of which Corporal Lewkowski has sent to you. I can attest to the fact that Corporal Lewkowski has in fact attended all training listed. For further verification, a training record is also kept and certified with the Alaska Police Standards Council.

Sergeant Steve Kalwara
Juneau Police Department
210 Admiral Way
Juneau, Alaska 99801

Signed by Sergeant Steve Kalwara.

When I left JPD in 1986, I was highly recommended to pursue a position with a drug unit in Northeast Ohio. It was with deep regret that I left JPD, but family matters were an issue, as my wife's mother was not well and we needed to be with her. I will always be proud of the fact that I was a corporal, a commissioned Alaska State Trooper and a member of the SWAT Team.

I resigned from the department on June 6, 1986.

CHAPTER SEVEN

NORTHEAST OHIO NARCOTICS AGENCY

I LEFT JUNEAU, ALASKA, AFTER ELEVEN years to take a position as an agent with a county narcotics unit in Northeast, Ohio. My wife's mother was ill with Alzheimer's disease, and my wife wanted to help care for her. That was the main reason we left Alaska, a place we had come to love. This decision would result in the worst career move of my life.

We sold our beautiful home, boat, and other property before returning to Ohio. The Juneau Police Department held a farewell party for me, presenting me with gifts, including my badge encased in a frame along with our department patches. I also received a beautiful panoramic photo of Juneau. I was sad to be leaving Alaska, which I had learned to love. Toni was ecstatic about returning home, and I was happy for her. She deserved to go home to be with her family and her mother after all these years. We packed our belongings and shipped them to our new rental home in Ohio. We took the Alaska Ferry to Prince Rupert and, from there, drove back home to Ohio.

The trip back was uneventful, except for one incident. It was evening and we were traveling on the expressway about forty miles west of Cleveland when a truck hauling large pieces of steel began to lose its load. Luckily, traffic was light. Five or six large pieces of steel came bouncing toward my car. I managed to avoid the steel as it hurtled toward us, ripping up pieces of the roadway. After all those miles traveled, this happens close to our destination!

My goal in life was to remain in law enforcement. I came highly recommended for my new position by a local police chief who was also a member of the drug agency's board of directors. I believed that if he recommended me, all would be well. I have known the chief personally since we were teenagers; my foster father was his uncle. I believed that I had no reason to research the position any more thoroughly than I had because of his recommendation. I also assumed the hiring director was a credible person. I did not know that politics would entangle me in its web of deceit and dishonesty. My need to return to Ohio and to have a job that I loved, coupled with the chief's recommendation, lulled me into a false sense of security. Or maybe I was just naive. I tried, in the last chapter, to acquaint the reader with my credentials, experience, and attitude toward law enforcement. This would all come into question in my new job.

My first day working for the drug unit was July 1, 1986, at nine am. Had I known what was coming, I would never have quit my job in Juneau. I would have first asked for a leave of absence to check it out. I sold my home, my boat and gave up my retirement to take this job. I placed my trust in the law enforcement community I was about to enter.

I reported for duty on schedule. I met with the director of the unit and learned that I would be working undercover assignments. This was a surprise, as this had not come up during interviews. I had been led to believe that I would be helping the agency target higher levels in drug organizations. The director gave me a copy of an employee's manual, and I read part of it that day.

The first day I arrived at work, much to my surprise, I was asked to sign a probationary consent form. I quit my position in Alaska never knowing about this condition before accepting the position, nor was it provided with any of the paperwork I signed. I did not know that I could be fired *without cause*! I would never have left a secure position with my previous department, nor would my wife have given up her job with the State of Alaska, to return here and work as a probationary employee. I later learned that several of the chief's friends on the board thought this up after my arrival. Somehow word had spread that the chief, who recommended me for this position, had made the comment that I would be running the agency within a year. I knew nothing of that, nor did I aspire to lead the agency. I knew I was in deep trouble when I learned that the director had heard about the chief's comments. The chief who recommended me sat on the board of this agency. It is apparent that this chief was not a friend of the director's, and I was being used as a foil in their political war.

I did not realize that I was hired as an undercover operative, but the director advised me early on that I would be working undercover indefinitely as he saw fit. Again, I was expecting to work drug investigations using the tried and true techniques that I had been trained on in Alaska. Now I found out that I would be required to come to the office and punch a time clock before and after my shift! Do what? I felt that punching the clock in and out was a dangerous position to place me in; drug dealers could follow me back to the office! Why not just wear a uniform? I became extremely cautious when coming to or from the office. This procedure could be dangerous, especially after finding out that I would be alone on these assignments with zero backup. These procedures were not how a professional drug unit functioned. Officer safety did not appear to be a priority in this agency.

I learned that my assignment consisted of sitting in an assigned bar for eight hours. I was not allowed to leave or even venture off as circumstances might dictate. Again, this was not what I considered a smart tactic. What could be more suspicious than sitting there for eight hours at a time?

FIRST FEW WEEKS ON DRUG UNIT

The first several weeks of employment I am writing from memory; I was not yet documenting my activity.

My first week at work, the director's wife drove me to Columbus to get a false driver's license; she was also an agent for the unit! The lieutenant of the unit was my direct supervisor and reported to the director; I did not know that the unit director's wife was also an agent. I was uncomfortable during the ride to Columbus. My gut instinct was that a boss's wife did not fit my ideal of a narcotics partner. The boss's wife! I was curious why the agency's controlling board of directors allowed this clear conflict of interest. In hindsight, I believe that this should have been my first real clue that something was not right with this agency.

Prior to the July 4th holiday weekend approaching, I was given a tour of the area that I would be working. The lieutenant and another agent were my tour guides. I did not know that before my hiring, the director had hired the lieutenant from his former department. They had both worked together for years and were best friends. The other agents in the unit were very bitter about this arrangement— another conflict of interest. After my hire, the director circulated a memo throughout the department saying that I was an experienced narcotics investigator who would be working to get to a higher-level source of the drugs infesting this county. On July 4th, 5th and 6th, I spent the holiday weekend off duty.

In Alaska, our drug officers followed strict protocols designed to be effective while providing maximum safety for the officers, especially any who might be working undercover. We conducted surveillance together, as safety for everyone was a major issue. We mainly used CIs (confidential informants) rather than undercover officers to be our eyes and ears within the suspect environment. This was done to lessen the greater risk of using undercover officers. Our team depended on each other and worked together for maximum effectiveness. I sensed right away that, in this organization, I would not experience the closeness and friendships I had developed with my team in Alaska. I know that I had discussed with the director of this unit, prior to taking this job, how we worked as a team. The director told me that this unit worked the same way. This was not true, as time would prove otherwise.

I began purchasing illicit drugs within the first weeks of my undercover work, but we had no strategy to reach the drug leadership. I was hired to get to higher levels in the drug gang hierarchy but was never asked to participate in strategic planning or to help develop tactical plans. I was truly shocked at the level of incompetency and unprofessionalism in the leadership of this "drug unit."

I was warned by other agents to "watch my back" and to "not trust anyone in the agency." I was also told to not trust the director's wife! Again, I cannot express how wrong this situation was; morale in this unit was lousy.

A female agent asked me to meet with her and some others behind a shopping center on my way to my assignment. I met them and they told me that the unit's regulations manual was a joke; they were getting a raw deal and were forming a union. They asked me if I would be willing to sign up for this union activity. Hell, I had just got here. They said they were hiring a lawyer; they were afraid of losing their jobs, and that it was the director's way or the highway. Obviously, I was entangled in a profoundly serious mess and regretted that I was hired from afar and had no way of knowing how bad the situation was with my new employer.

During my first few weeks with the agency, I felt depressed and frustrated with the lack of effective communication or supervision. These are essential elements of running a team, especially one engaged in a dangerous job such as drug law enforcement.

I decided to call the chief who had recommended me for this job to tell him of the situation. I had no one else to call for help. I was alone with no guidance. I made the call and continued to communicate with him weekly. He advised me to begin documenting events. He also suggested that I ask the lieutenant to evaluate my progress regularly, as I was new and wanted to be sure that I was on the right track.

I asked my lieutenant to do this, but he never would meet with me to discuss my performance. The only comments he made to me were, "You're doing a good job." I told the director of the lieutenant's decision not to meet with me weekly. The director's secretary told me when he heard of my hire, he slammed his briefcase on his desk and shouted, "Why the hell is this chief telling me who to hire?" The director felt that I was there to spy on him, which was not true. I had no knowledge of any of this.

One of my assigned bars was a biker-type bar, and again, I had to stay in the bar for my entire shift. I sipped on beer the best I could for eight hours. I was never a heavy drinker and rarely drank hard liquor. Eventually some of the bikers started buying me shots of whiskey. I could not dump them out because they would down the shots in front of one another. I made the director aware of this so that he could understand my situation. I was told by the director of the unit to drink only Perrier water or pop! I know that this is hard to believe, as common sense would dictate that this was absurd. I doubt that any of them had ever worked undercover in a biker bar. Let them try to sit there for eight hours and drink Perrier water! I guarantee that purchasing drugs under these conditions would be considered very suspicious at best. The director and his lieutenant did not listen to anything I had to say, and it was clear that I would not receive the supervisory help that I requested. Understand, that having come from a drug unit that was professional and integrated into a team, this unit was a nightmare.

This poor supervision was not what I expected as a new employee. I knew that I was being set up to get hurt or to be fired from this job. I worked alone while another agent was assigned to bars at the opposite end of the county. This made absolutely no sense whatsoever! The frustration and depression I felt I cannot put into words. The position I was in was destroying me. I was in a state of shock, and I had no one to turn to for help. So, in desperation, I wrote a letter to the agency's board of directors requesting a confidential meeting with them to discuss the problems I was finding. They denied my request. I was familiar with the chain of command, but when the Lieutenant and Director would not talk to me, I had to go over their heads.

The other agents were shaking in their boots, afraid for their jobs. I had a look at the unit's caseload for the prior year; I did not find any major drug busts, just thirty-five small cases with no major arrests. This was a well-funded agency that was doing nothing for the community.

The agency was governed by a board of directors, which I suspect had no members with narcotics experience. The board was not providing proper oversight, in my opinion. Nepotism, favoritism, lack of supervision, and no working strategy for success were all obvious to me, a new employee. A real board would have drained this swamp, but I saw no sign that they were interested.

On my first cocaine buy, I returned to the office with the evidence and to write my report. I did not have any idea of their report procedures, so I proceeded with I was used to doing in my past unit. I finished writing the report and asked a fellow agent where I needed to place the report to be typed. I was told that we must type our own reports. I could type with two fingers, so I typed out the report. I later received a written reprimand stating that I had asked the female agent to type my report. The female agent agreed that this was not true. The written reprimands had begun. The director told me that he didn't care if I had to work overtime to complete it or if it took all night to type my report. I complied with his order. I was told by the other agents that the secretary employed by the agency is an Executive Secretary and only types for the director or lieutenant.

On July 16, approximately ten days after I started, the lieutenant wrote a memo to the director regarding six points of discussion he stated he had with me. One point stated that my activity sheets were not filled out as instructed. I was only filling out the sheets as the other agents advised me to. Another point he made was that I felt it was not necessary to fill out these reports, and that I did not feel they trusted me, as they were having me punch the time clock. Again, he was not listening to me; I talked to him on several other occasions that I was concerned for agent safety. He was not listening to my concerns. I discussed the situation with other agents who thought what they were doing was not only unsafe but absurd. I discussed with the lieutenant the problems we agents were having. The lieutenant said that I was the one who stated that backup was not necessary. Say WHAT? He never listened to me the entire time I was at the agency. Again, I was being advised by the other agents not to trust anyone. It would be obvious to any experienced narcotics agent that this so-called unit did not operate as a team in any manner.

The agents that I was involved with were scared to death of the lieutenant and the director. Agents advised me that the director was opening their mail. He claimed that I did nothing but gripe to him since the day I was employed by the agency. In my wildest dreams I would never have guessed what would happen to me in this agency after being highly recommended for the position.

On July 22, I again attempted to talk with the lieutenant, but he would not listen to me. On July 23, I bought more cocaine with no surveillance or backup. They had no tactics to trace these drugs to their source, just evidence for small-time arrests.

Before July 24, I was told by the unit's Sergeant that drug activity was taking place in a bar on the way to the other bar that I usually worked. On this rare occasion, I was wired, with two agents outside monitoring the conversation. I stopped at the suspect bar and began a conversation with the bartender. He led me to believe that he could sell me some cocaine. I arranged to buy cocaine from the bartender the following Monday. This was the first time I had other agents with me on a buy.

I returned to the office to advise the lieutenant and the director. I was shocked when I was told not to go to that bar again; "*it's a waste of time.*" I could not believe this! I have never been told to ignore a felony case. This bar was near a plant under construction where drug activity was rampant. All the agents acknowledged that no other police unit was working at or near this bar, so it was not a matter of us interfering with another unit's work. I wrote on my activity sheet that I was told to stay away from this bar. The director went into a rage when he read my report and accused me of *grandstanding*! I previously was told to make my activity sheet as accurate and detailed as possible. I later learned that others on the board may have been privy to looking at my activity sheets. I was now totally aware that I was being set up for termination during my probationary period. I kept my cool during this incident as I remembered I'd only been there a few weeks.

ALASKA COURT SUBPOENA

After just a few weeks with this agency, I was subpoenaed to appear in court in Juneau, Alaska, to testify in some drug cases in which I was the control officer for a CI. I was flown back to Alaska, happy to have a chance to discuss my new job with my prior team.

The first trial concluded on August 1st; the jury returned a guilty verdict. It was now possible for me to go back to Ohio, but the other trials would start on August 5th. The DA's office decided to hold me over for the remaining trials instead of flying me back to Ohio only to return. I received a per diem of $80 during my stay. When I finally returned to Ohio, the director refused to pay me for the working days that I was away from our office. The (Alaskan) district attorney sent my current director a letter stating that in his ten years as a DA, no other agency ever denied paying a public officer to testify in court for criminal cases. He further stated that the director should not penalize me for being a good police officer and testifying on many of the cases that I had closed in Juneau.

Upon my return, I was told by other agents that during my absence, the director and lieutenant commented that I was in Alaska goofing off. Without my testimony in court, six major drug dealers would have gone free. All were found guilty to the charges against them. I lost wages, as I was never paid by the director for this time.

In my absence, the director held a hearing regarding the report writing incident. The hearing note stated that I had asked the female agent to type my first report. She had attested to the fact that I *did not ask her*, but she was not even called to the hearing. The other point he made at this hearing was that I was not to report to work until ten minutes of my starting time. I was accused of having problems with the rules. All the subjects the director discussed at the hearing I had discussed with the lieutenant days prior. Other agents had never heard of so many hearings in such a short time. They all agreed that I was being set up. I never received any guidance or any help from the lieutenant, even after asking to have weekly meetings with him to discuss my job performance. I never dreamed that our personal discussions held in the office would be used in a hearing.

I had five years of experience as a shift supervisor in Alaska where I regularly performed evaluations of police officers. I had attended several classes on writing evaluations and proper supervision. Prior to being in law enforcement, I was in management positions for many years dealing with people and employees. What was happening to me was not in any rule books about proper evaluation of police personnel. Agents were telling me daily that I was being set up for termination during probation. I was fully aware of what was happening. But I had no one to help me. I was alone, and, in the meantime, I was doing my job. I was buying drugs, typing my reports and following the rules as instructed. Agents advised me that no one in seven years or so had infiltrated the bars as effectively as I had done in just a few weeks. In my prior job, I did not sit in bars for an entire shift, as we used CIs to perform this task. We monitored our informant's activities outside and were ready in case the CI needed immediate backup. I was not subjected to have to drink for eight hours of time—not drink the whole time but be in there for the entire eight hours. The director also advised me, prior to starting this job, that they worked the same way that we did in Alaska. That statement was not true. Every time I asked the lieutenant how I was doing, he would reply, "You are doing a great job, Lewk."

Things began getting worse for all the agents. The lieutenant sent out a memo stating that no agent is to go to any police department in the county without being ordered to do so. Now, police officers that work the street are one of the best sources of information about drug activity, and it is good policy to talk with them to gain local intelligence. We were being told to stay away from this type of information! What could possibly be the reason for this?

On August 8, I was called in for a meeting with the lieutenant to discuss the purpose of punching a time clock while undercover. I told him of the danger involved, but he would not listen. I asked him if I could call another agent to retrieve my evidence and return it to the office, this way I would not risk the chance of being followed. He did not listen very well, nor did he respond to that idea. I was told that I could not report to work until ten minutes before my starting time. I abided by their rules. Now, this whole discussion was held in the lieutenant's office as if we were talking one-on-one. I never showed any disrespect and followed the rules. I now have worked a few weeks for this agency. Things seemed to me to be moving quickly toward my termination. The lieutenant called a hearing in the director's office to discuss my meeting with the lieutenant. I was quite shocked that my first private conversation with the lieutenant would turn into a hearing!

I recall leaving the biker bar one night feeling no pain. While driving back to the office *to punch out*, I was stopped by a state trooper and pulled over. The trooper asked me if I had been drinking. I said that I had been, and he asked for my license. I asked him, "My real one or my fake one?"

He looked at me and said, "*You work for the drug unit.*"

I replied, "Yes."

He further told me that I should quit as the unit was not worth a shit. I told him I that could make it home as I lived close by, and he gratefully sent me on my way.

On several occasions, the lieutenant saw me reading the memos he sent to me and noticed that I was reading the comments that he made to me in the hearing. The lieutenant told me to put them away as they were not important. Don't worry about them? Don't worry about the lies; I'm just being set up for dismissal. Why did he write them if he did not want me to read them?

I purchased cocaine several times in a short period, and the lieutenant would tell me what a good job I was doing. Other agents told me that they were afraid to say anything—afraid that they would lose their jobs. They were concerned that when they purchased drugs, they had no backup or communications with anyone. I personally never observed anyone conduct a proper surveillance in the time I was with the agency. Any experienced narcotics investigator that conducted surveillance would state that surveillance was the key factor in drug busts.

I'll never forget the one kid from whom I started buying cocaine. I purchased drugs from him at least three times. He would take me to an adjoining county to buy the cocaine. I drove to the location and obtained intelligence information while waiting outside. I would collect addresses, car descriptions and license plate numbers. I kept a quart of beer under my seat from which I would pour some on me prior to the kid getting in the car. He thought I was really loaded and kept on yelling at me to use some of the cocaine. I refused, telling him that I was an ex-addict and used the cocaine I was purchasing to trade with my cleaning ladies for sex. He then accused me of being a cop. I pulled the car over to the side of the road and yanked him out of the car. I slammed him against the door and told him me never to call me a cop again.

I made several buys from this long-haired kid when I decided it was a good time to "roll him over" (recruit him as a CI). I approached the lieutenant with this idea, since the reason I was hired was to get to the higher level of drug dealers, not just arrest low-level runners. He and the director thought it was not a good idea. I then advised them that we should at least contact the other county sheriff to advise them of the situation. Both the lieutenant and the director also nixed this idea.

The kicker came when I told the lieutenant that the kid had decided to join the Marines, and that this was a good opportunity for us to roll him. The lieutenant said, "FUCK HIM, LET'S LET HIM JOIN THE MARINES. WE WILL BUST HIM AFTER HIS TRAINING!" The next time I saw the kid, he had his hair cut and was telling me how excited he was to join the Marines. He vowed that he was not going to sell anymore or use drugs.

The lieutenant's comments made me sicker than I already was. What an outfit I was working for; what were we accomplishing? What were our goals? I thought it was to get a higher level of drug dealers. This kid could have helped us bust a major drug ring prior to joining the Marines. I asked for surveillance on this major dealer, but I never got it. Instead I was told to stay out of the bar that I had been buying cocaine in.

Prior to my being hired, the director of the unit told me that the case officer, which would be me, would have a say as to how cases proceeded. This statement was totally untrue. He did not want me to succeed with the investigation but instead wanted to destroy a kid's life. This was the director's answer to the drug war.

The agents I worked with in Alaska were shocked when I told them my story. These comments made by the director and lieutenant were totally out of line with my law enforcement training and personal morals.

In late August, I was warned for leaving work early. That was the night I typed my letter of resignation. I came to work early the next day to talk to the director. I was told by the lieutenant that he did not want to talk to me. I had not eaten lunch while on duty and was going to ask how much time to spend for lunch and did I have to punch a time clock for lunch. I did not get an answer.

After being told to stay away from the two bars where I was buying drugs in or expected to buy drugs, I again drafted a letter to the board of directors' committee that oversaw the drug agency. I asked for a meeting with them to be held without the director of the drug unit present. I attempted to go through the chain of command, but to no avail. I asked the board for the opportunity to speak with them and was turned down.

The director and the lieutenant felt that I could continue to stay in the bars on my eight-hour shifts and drink pop and Perrier water. I did not think when I was hired that alcohol was a requirement of my job when I was in redneck biker bars. Obviously, alcohol is unhealthy and dangerous to do on a nightly basis, but it is also ignorant and immoral. I was advised by a physician that I not drink alcohol. I would not have cared if I were able to exit the bar and perhaps go to another bar or move around more.

The worst part of all this was what was happening to me personally. I was arriving home every night half shit-faced with no one to turn to, depressed and totally did not have control of my life. I was losing it. There was really no one besides Toni, my wife, to talk to about all of this. She was very sympathetic, as she knew me as a strong person who could handle anything life dished out. I was a survivor, and I always will be. I never took any crap from anyone after leaving the orphanage. I was married at sixteen years old and raised a family without help. I worked in the retail grocery business at age sixteen and worked my way up to meat manager. I had owned a convenience store, had a commercial pilot license with instrument rating, multi-engine and was a flight instructor. In Alaska, I was a good police officer and was respected by the public. The DA's office, in the cases I initiated, thought I was a good person and dedicated to law enforcement. I was extremely aggressive in the narcotics unit and made good cases against major drug dealers. Now my reputation, credibility, honesty and everything I worked for in my life was being destroyed by a man that was afraid I was after his job. It seemed unfair that after forty-six years of being an honest, hard-working individual, that this man could destroy me in a matter of weeks. This community was where I was raised, attended school, and resided. He was an outsider from another county. I have never been at a lower point my life as I was with this agency. This was not me, as others that know me will attest.

I finally decided to write a letter of resignation. I could not work under these conditions. I called the chief who had recommended me for the position and told him what I was about to do; he advised me to rescind the letter of resignation. I took his advice, although I was constantly in touch by phone with this chief; however, he never really backed me up.

The director of the unit did not hide his disdain for me. On August 19, he told me, "I had a gut feeling when I met you that you would not make it. I formed that opinion in three days, and I should not have hired you in the first place. The only reason you were hired was because your friend, the chief, recommended you. Your record with your previous department means nothing to me; I do not want to hear about it again. You will fail." I told him that I had never failed in my life at anything I had ever done and was not about to now. He further stated, "We will send all the agents into the bars." I didn't think this was true, as he did not send the director's wife or close friend of his, who was an alcoholic, into bars. He also told me in essence, "You will probably be on probation for a year, and I know other agents who were working in bars for seven years. They handle their drinking problems."

I was not hired as a liquor agent, nor was I hired to spend time in bars my entire shift. During this meeting, I could not reply to the ignorant and humiliating things the director was saying. I was angry inside but held my anger back and was not insubordinate. My wife was fully aware that I would usually not tolerate any man speaking to me in that manner. I was not sure of my feelings. I knew that I was going to be without a job in law enforcement. That scared me, as I could not return to my previous department. I did not know what was going to happen to me and felt that I was in a dangerous position, unsure of my own safety. I began to wear my bullet-resistant vest while working undercover. I also took the 38-caliber pistol they gave me and placed it under the seat of my car. I began carrying my Colt .45 on my person.

I called the guys I worked with in Alaska, as they had expressed concern for my safety. One of them was even willing to come to Ohio to assist me while others advised me to watch my back. I knew that the director of the unit resented the chief's recommendation to hire me, but I did not know how or when I would be fired. I knew that the director did not want to hire me. I was done before I even started working for this agency. I knew they did not want me to succeed in this position. We could have arrested two major drug dealers in the very short time I was there but did not even try. I suppose that they did not want me to succeed. Politics in the county were nasty with lots of infighting between Democrats and Republicans. This was affecting this agency.

MY SITUATION WORSENS

September 5, 1986, I once again asked the lieutenant if I was doing okay with my assignments. He said that there were no problems he was aware of; "You're doing a good job." All this time, he continued to stick the knife in my back. He wrote another letter to the director regarding this conversation. He wrote that he had informed me that when I made drug buys, I was to set them up for the following night. That way I could wear a wire and have backup. The lieutenant wrote that I never worked this way and that I did not think it was necessary to have backup. This is what I had been asking for all along! I was the one to suggest these things. He completely turned the tables on me again after telling me I was doing a good job. Why was he concocting these stories to tell the director? Well, it was obvious to me he was setting me up for failure.

I read an article in the narcotics officers' magazine dated September and October 1986. The article was written by the past director of the New York Bureau of Narcotics, retired. He wrote:

"Drug enforcement is a specialized area of law enforcement and is considered one of the most dangerous areas but has indicated the retaliatory measures recently being experienced has made drug enforcement riskier than ever. Drug enforcement has always been regarded as one of the most frustrating areas of law enforcement, and, often, the risks and accomplishments of our dedicated officers go unnoticed. State and local

objectives require that law enforcement resources be directed to stopping local drug distribution drug use and drug related crimes."

I had hoped the lieutenant, director, and executive committee had read that article, as they certainly had not accomplished goals or even understood drug law enforcement. Nor had that agency served the people's demands to conduct a real drug war.

I was assigned to spend my time in several new bars that were close to one another. On my first evening, I became very sick and did not return to the office. I went directly home and to bed. I awoke at seven am the next morning and visited a doctor. The doctor advised me to stop drinking alcohol, and my wife called the lieutenant to advise him that I would not be at work.

When I returned to the office, I was discussing the doctor's report with the lieutenant when I heard the director shout, "Let him drink Perrier water!" Now let me assure you that I am a healthy individual, and in every position I have had since age sixteen, I don't remember ever calling in sick to work. I work out daily and had for years. I have worked since I was thirteen years old and am not known as a sickly person.

Most experienced narcotics officers laugh at the idea of sitting in a bar for eight hours at a time working undercover, drinking pop or Perrier water. I doubt that the bar I was working in ever served Perrier water. I did ask the director how long I would be undercover with this agency. I felt that was a fair question that I had a right to ask.

He answered me in a rage, stating, "A year or two, or indefinitely; I run this agency not you." If I would have been told that, as a new employee, I would be working undercover for a reasonable amount of time, I would have accepted that decision. However, I would not have accepted working eight hours in a bar indefinitely. I was hired as a Special Drug Agent, not an undercover specialist. However, none of this mattered, as they were setting me up to be fired before I started.

The lieutenant advised me that the director was mad about me leaving work the night I was sick without calling anyone. The director was going to dock my pay for this. I told the lieutenant that I was not told that I was supposed to call anyone at 11:30 pm at night. I did not want to wake anyone, as I had only two-and-a-half hours to go. I was the only agent working in the county. No one knew where I was, and obviously, no one was concerned for my safety. I talked with a female agent who had been there for years, and she did not know what procedure to follow if she became sick at that time of the night. However, another hearing was held in reference to my sick leave. I was suspended for three days. I wrote a letter of grievance to the director, stating it was unfair and unjust to be suspended.

I had been given a copy of everyone's pager number when I was hired. Working in a so-called undercover position in the bars, I did not keep a copy of agent's pagers with me or in my vehicle. I did keep a copy after I was suspended for three days. The director answered my letter and advised me never to leave my assigned area without notifying a supervisor. What would this "supervisor" do if an agent had to leave a bar? Nothing is the answer. It was around September 1986 that I hired a lawyer to represent me, as it was soon time that I would be terminated.

While working in the one bar I was assigned to daily, I talked to the bar owner a lot. We talked quite a bit at times, as we were often the only ones in the bar. I made up a story that I was a supervisor for a cleaning company, and the cleaning women used a lot of drugs that they purchased from me. Now this owner, I was told, had contacts with organized crime. I was trying to get higher up the drug food chain by gaining this guy's trust.

I was a member of a local gym where I worked out as I have done most of my life. One day while I was on my back lifting weights, I looked up and saw the owner of the bar that I was working in looking down at me. I had never seen him in this gym before. I believed that he lived on the other side of the county. He walked over and shook my hand. Now it had been several days since I had been in his bar. My real name was on the sign-up sheet in the gym lobby; the bar owner only knew my undercover "work" name. While he was at the gym, I was able to change my sign-in sheet using my fake name. I felt my position at the bar was now compromised and called the lieutenant to advise him of this turn of events. It was obvious to me that the director and lieutenant chose not to believe me.

The next day I was leaving for work when I noticed my wife frantically waving at me. I thought she was waving goodbye. I later found out that she had observed a vehicle acting suspiciously in our neighborhood. My wife described the female who was driving the car. I discovered that this female was the bar owner's wife, and I later identified her vehicle. My suspicions at the gym were correct; the guy was checking up on me.

After telling the lieutenant about this incident, he recommended that I still go back to the bar, and he further said, if the bar owner were smart that he would quote "club me." My thoughts were that the bar owner would attempt to harm me, and that backup was necessary, especially that night. I was by myself and survived the night. The lieutenant was going to send a female agent into the bar to see if she could find out how the owner felt about me. I don't believe he ever did.

The other agent on duty across town was quite upset about being in bars the entire shift, complaining to me often that he was not feeling well. Another agent who worked part-time was from the same department the lieutenant and director were from. We discussed our assignments with him. He thought it was foolish, and he talked with the lieutenant about the situation. The lieutenant laughed him off and thought it was funny. The other full-time agent told me that he did not go into the bars until nine pm, and if the county wanted to pay him $12 an hour to screw off, he would do so. He felt that he was not accomplishing anything at all. Now, remember, I was buying cocaine in the early weeks of my employment. It was obvious to me that no one in this agency was doing anything productive at all. All one had to do was look at the caseload for 1986. When I did get a look at it, I believe I saw thirty-five minor drug cases for the year. Nothing that an ordinary rookie patrolman could not have accomplished. I can say that without hesitation. I was assigned to another bar on the east side of the county and told to spend my entire shift there. I was also asked to wear my assigned ball cap in the bar always. The stated reason for the cap was so that other undercover cops would be able to ID me. That way they could monitor my activities or have conversations with me while working in a crowded bar. I did not wear the hat, as I knew it was for the off-duty cops from his former department whom he had hired to set me up. I was also given a new schedule, so that I could accommodate the director's friends. My new schedule was from for to twelve pm, and the bar I was assigned to had once been a biker bar but now was a haven for older men. There was not a lot of activity to report. I was dealing with older guys who liked to get drunk and sing. I called in sick one evening from this bar as no one was there.

I knew that I was being watched by off-duty cops, so I started to ask several of my own friends and relatives into the bars as witnesses. I never sat with them, nor did I buy them drinks on county money. They were there to watch, observe, and be witnesses if necessary.

One night shortly after starting in this bar, a guy came in wearing shiny black shoes. I looked him in the eye and said you look like a cop I used to know. I went to the phone to advise my attorney what I was up against. I told him the cop is out of his jurisdiction and spying on me, affecting my ability to perform my job. I was terribly upset and told the attorney I was going to beat the crap out of the guy. He advised me not to, and I took his advice. On September 24, another cop came in the bar from the director's old department. He reported to the director that I was at the bar wearing a Coors T-shirt with the word Coors written on the front of the shirt. He noted I was wearing a hunting cap and drinking two Miller light beers. He had the wrong guy; I did not drink Miller beer or wear a Coors T-shirt. These so-called police officers testified later, at my last hearing, to what they saw. He swore to that statement that was totally not true; he had identified the wrong person. It didn't really matter, as everything that was said about me was lies.

I had no protection from the beginning as employment in Ohio is an employment-at-will state. That is why I was placed on probation upon my arrival at the agency and not told before I arrived in Ohio. After resigning from my department in Alaska and having sold my home, everything I worked for was lost. I did not even own a home in Ohio but was expecting to purchase the one I was living in. A bank would not loan money to a person without a job. My wife and I were at the lowest point in our lives. I also had two granddaughters in our home along with my daughter living with us. I had owned a house before I was twenty-one, owned another beautiful home in this county, and a beautiful home in Alaska. Now I will be out of law enforcement and without a job. I was spending my last working days as a cop being watched and set up. I was attempting to perform my job, which was to purchase drugs. I was not allowed to do that. There was no drug activity in this bar, it was only a convenient place to spy on me and my activity. I later learned that these off-duty people watching me rented an apartment right across from the bar that I was assigned to daily.

On September 24, 1986, I contacted the senior agent, as I was hungry, and he told me to go to lunch. I called my wife to ask her to meet me at the McDonalds about two miles from the bar I was working. I told her I would park my county car and meet her at the pizza shop on the corner. I parked my car and met my wife.

The lieutenant and another cop friend of his had followed me that night and watched me meet my wife. I had entered my wife's car after a short time that evening. They later reported to the newspaper that I met with an unknown female in a white Lincoln town car after leaving my assigned area. It would appear to anyone reading the article that I had left the bar to maybe meet a hooker. Now they had the plate number off the white Lincoln, and it was all white with a leather top, probably the only one around like it. If they would have run the plate, they would have known it was my wife who was the unknown female, but that was not printed in the paper.

Another incident to make me look bad; I had the approval of a senior agent to have the lunch with my wife. If I were investigating a fellow cop, it would have been conducted in a professional and detailed manner. In my case, it was lie after lie. But they won the battle; I never had a chance. No friends, no chief, nowhere to turn—I was alone in this agency.

I sat and drank beer with this cop friend of the director who was hired to follow me. I later was curious whether he was being paid out of buy money funds or cash. He drove off to speak with the lieutenant and later told the lieutenant that we drank seven or eight beers before leaving the bar. He did not know that I had two witnesses in the bar watching him and me. I did not drink seven or eight beers.

I felt threatened and could not possibly do my job. It was useless to continue the assigned task, which was to locate sources of illegal drugs. I learned later that the reason the director had given to place me in the bar was to obtain information about an arsonist who had killed several people. That might be true, but I was never given any intelligence information about this and knew nothing about it! What is the sense undercover surveillance where the officer is unaware of these important details?

At times, I would leave my assigned area to follow up on drug activity supplied to me by patrons of the bar. I felt that was part of my job, and I had witnesses to testify on my behalf that when I left the bar I was following up on leads. They were not given the chance to testify for me. If the cops hired by the director of the unit would have followed me more often, they would have seen evidence of my efforts to do my job.

One of the hired goons told the lieutenant that he entered the bar at 7:50 pm and left at 12:30 am and that he spent $10 at the bar. He stated that I drank eleven beers while I was sitting next to him. He only spent $10. If I'm not mistaken, the money supplied to me by this agency was only $20 to $30, and I always accounted for my expenses. There was no way I drank eleven beers—totally wrong. More lies. It was no longer a case of me doing my job; it was a case of survival. Two others of our agents compiled a list of things they were concerned about, including the lack of trust in this agency. Their list consisted of about seventy items. The senior agent and I presented them to the executive board. To my knowledge, nothing has ever been done to address the problems. One afternoon, I was invited to meet with the union rep along with the other two agents. I was advised by the union rep that the consulting firm for the county told the director not to do anything to me now, as it could cause problems with union negotiations. I feel as if I were being blamed by the director for bringing in the union. I was trying to survive; I was not involved with the union.

I was told again to wear the assigned hat all the time. A barmaid I came to know from talking with her when the bar was slow commented to me about a patron at the end of the bar drinking a soda pop. She told me, "He's drinking pop. Why does he come in here and not drink alcohol?" So much for the director's crazy theory that I should be drinking Perrier water, right?

Another evening I identified the cops that were watching me in the bar, and I mentioned it to the barmaid. I told her they were both narcotics cops and to be careful. This would help build up my credibility, as I was in there every night. The cop friends of the director were drinking beer, why not Perrier water? Their expense money came from the same place as mine. I felt more threatened; more and more cops following cops! What have I done to deserve this treatment? Surveillance on me? Can you believe that? I haven't seen any surveillance on known drug dealers since I've been in this agency.

One weekend evening, the bar was very crowded. I was bowling on the bowling machine with an off-duty barmaid. Two more females arrived as I went to buy the off-duty barmaid a drink. A tall male came into the crowded bar, which was elbow to elbow. I had never seen this guy before, and he appeared to be intoxicated, as his voice carried across the entire bar. He got very close to me and rubbed the side of my waist with his arm. He felt the weapon concealed under my jacket, and he began to shout in a loud voice that I had a weapon. I attempted to quiet him down, but I could not. I saw him walk toward the telephone. This was another set up. I find it quite odd that a man I had never seen in the bar before would come right up to me in this crowded bar and feel my concealed weapon. I knew he was calling the police. He had made the call, and about fifteen minutes later they arrived with a police dog. I was led away in handcuffs and arrested. I advised the officer while he was cuffing me that I was a police officer working narcotics at the station. He called my superior, and I was released and taken back to the same bar. While outside the bar, prior to being cuffed, the police officer stated to a few patrons of the bar, "It's okay, he is a narcotics cop." I was shocked when they took me back to the same bar. I was quite surprised they would do that. I explained to the owner that I was bailed out. A male subject who was sitting with the bar owner told me that he would testify that I had done nothing wrong. I left the bar and returned to my home.

The next day I was asked to write a report on the incident. I wrote the report and asked for a change of assignments. I was at the lowest point in my life. Having only worked for this agency for a short time, my life was being destroyed, and I could do nothing to save me from what I knew was going to happen. I was dealing with two monsters: a director with no scruples and a lieutenant to back him up. I later learned that this director, when he was with his old department, destroyed several other good officers. A captain in the director's old department heard about my plight and stated that I must have been a good police officer if the director had me terminated.

The two other agents I was working with continued to tell me that no one had ever been exposed to the many hearings I had. The senior agent told me that the director's wife went to tanning salons and hairdressers on agency time.

In later months, one of the agents acquired the director's wife's personal appointment book, and he gave it to me. I observed, personally, the many appointments she had scheduled on company time. I gave the book to a female reporter at the Plain Dealer, which was a big mistake. Instead of giving her a copy, I gave her the real thing. I was hoping they would provide proof about what was happening in this agency. Obviously, I wasn't thinking right at the time. I also saw prescriptions for Valium in the appointment book—for large quantities of Valium made out to her. I reported this to an individual who was a toxicologist. He told me that anyone with that amount Valium is either hooked on it or selling.

I contacted the reporter who told me that she misplaced the book and couldn't find it. What a fool I was. I can only say that in my state of mind, I was desperate and did not use my head. The senior agent told me that nobody records lunch on their activity sheets. I was written up for not signing out to lunch on my activity sheet. The senior agent also said that he told a director on the executive board that he was screwing off and not spending time in his assigned bar as he could not handle it anymore.

The lieutenant, nor his cop friends, ever attempted to follow me, as if they did, they would have discovered that I was getting drug information from several people. I was doing my job. I also wondered why he did not ask me where I was when he said he could not locate me, and I was not in my assigned area.

On October 24, I was given papers by the lieutenant referencing disciplinary action. He left the office and returned and asked me to resign. As this action would reflect upon my employment history, I advised him that I would not resign. I returned to the same bar for my assignment, and the director's cop friend and girlfriend were at the bar. The entire evening was spent talking to this guy and his girlfriend. He drank numerous beers while his girlfriend was drinking black Russians. He was trying to make conversation with me regarding poker games and weapons. The director knew that I played legal poker in Alaska and that I had a fully automatic, registered weapon. This off-duty cop was fully briefed on what to talk to me about.

October 25 I went back to the same bar awaiting my disciplinary hearing. There were two regulars in the bar, but otherwise it was completely empty. I returned to the office to punch the time clock. On October 28 I was back in the same bar where I had been arrested.

I ran out of expense money by 11:30. I called the lieutenant, but he said I must stay in the bar till two am. I called my wife to bring more of my own money.

I was assigned to another bar in the eastern part of the county. I was given information on some suspected drug activity. This was the first time that I was given any type of intelligence information from the sergeant or anyone else in this outfit.

The first night in the bar, I met the two suspects and bought them a beer. The next night they were not there, but I talked to, and met, other patrons. I also observed a drug deal taking place at the back of the bar near the pool table. I followed the person outside and got his license plate. I asked the lieutenant to run the plate, but I never received any information back from him.

Early on October 2, a hearing was held in the director's office. Present were the lieutenant, the sergeant, the director and me. The director asked me why I wanted a change of assignment. I had requested a change from bar duties, as I and others were concerned about being assigned to bars for eight hours. The director stated he did not understand why I wanted to make a change in duties. I pretty much must take orders, as he said that we run this organization, but you can offer a suggestion anytime you want. I replied that this was a suggestion, and how can I do a better job? I had no problem taking orders. The director replied, "You do have a problem taking orders. You have a line of bullshit forty miles long. This bar you are assigned to is where someone committed a triple murder. First time I heard about this! They burned a house down with three people inside and I thought you would come across with information, but I didn't want to pressure you. We just wanted you to go in there and listen. I didn't want to leave this on your shoulders. *You don't have to know what's going on.*"

I felt that it was his responsibility to let me know for my own safety, as we never had backup in this unit.

He continued, "It's a strange time to be asking for a change of duty assignment; I wouldn't dream of asking for a change unless I was working with someone for two years minimum."

I did not realize I would be working for two years in a bar, or I would not have accepted this assignment.

He continued, "You were given the duties, you have only been here for three months. I'm not happy with your performance. I'm not satisfied at all." (I was the only agent currently buying drugs, according to other agents. No one had infiltrated the bars I had been successful in). He continued, "I am at the point here where your probation is over, you are an ex-employee in my mind and toward the top of my mind all the time."

I replied that no one in the agency had told me that I was doing poorly. I said that I had requested weekly case evaluations from the lieutenant. He never met with me to discuss my cases, only to advise me weekly that I was doing a good job.

The director replied, "During probation I didn't see you as a good aggressive employee. I saw you goofing off, you are reluctant to take orders and I'm not happy with you as a probationary employee. If you had been here twenty years and had a bad month, that would be a different thing."

I could not last three months in a bar under the conditions he imposed. How could I last twenty years? I was not the only agent concerned about the situation.

He continued, "I'm always watching a probationary employee. I am watching their attitudes. I haven't seen a good attitude from you since you started."

I have only seen the director on a few occasions and never received any help or knowledge from the lieutenant in the days I had been there. I was excited on the three occasions when I purchased cocaine, but I was not allowed to continue my job to get to a higher source of the drugs.

The director continued, "You can drink, and you go home early, this doesn't sound like a healthy guy to me."

I think the last time I was sick was when I was flying an airplane back in 1968. I had a terrible headache, as I was piloting an airplane from New York to Cleveland. Luckily, I had another pilot on board.

The director continues, "I'm starting to make my determination. If you should stay in this organization, some action has to be taken to get you to be an aggressive employee. If you cannot you'll get termination papers because I'm not satisfied. That is as plain as I can make it. I am not too far from acting. You can say whatever you want." (He took this action on October 31, 1986). He continued, "Did you ever dream you would be in bars as a narcotics agent? You are the last man in, why wouldn't we use you? You're from Alaska; why can't you do a simple job like that? What can you do? It's that simple: you must do the job. I did not come looking for you. I never looked for you as an employee. I don't think this is a bad detail. I could send you out on shittier details. This place you're working has burglars and every criminal type in the world, including murderers." (First I had heard about that!) He continues, "We are trying to supply intelligence reports to the police community. The police requested that we go in there."

If I had been properly briefed, I would have been aware of what was involved and might have accomplished our objectives.

He continued, "It's up to you to come in, to come up with stories. Just give them a line of bullshit. If you can't, you are no good to us all. This is your problem; you must figure things out yourself. I can't do it for you. You can drink whatever you want to drink; you are in the narcotics business as part of the game. What you do in bars is your business. I'm not telling you how to do it. I'm telling you, you will go where you are assigned. If you don't like this type of work, the ball is in your court."

I later learned that the reason I was here was to spy on the director. Not true! I had received no assistance from my immediate supervisor, who would not listen to me or properly evaluate my progress. I believed that I was doing my job. I never had a problem infiltrating a bar and conversing with potential suspects. I had a letter from my lieutenant in Alaska stating that I was an excellent undercover operative, as I can talk about many of life's experiences as I had many times. I believe my superiors in Alaska would have attested to how much I liked narcotics work. My history of convictions working with my unit supported that. The Juneau DA's office at one time asked us to lay off, as we were flooding their office with narcotics cases. I am well informed on how an undercover officer should operate. Punching in and out for work is not only ignorant, it was setting an agent up for serious trouble. Everything that was being done in that agency was contrary to what I was taught and that the Drug Enforcement Agency would teach. This agency owned a $40,000 surveillance van that was not being used in any surveillance on any major drug dealers. I felt as if I were working as an informant and not an agent, as I worked alone with no backup or any communications.

One other agent on duty on the other side of the county admitted that all he did was screw off. In my opinion, this unit was a disgrace to the community it served. I have had very little contact with the sergeant in the agency, as he worked the day shift. He was aware of my situation; I even asked him for help to see what was going on with me or what I was doing wrong. I told him that I never had a disciplinary problem in my life. I was dumbfounded as to what was going on in this agency. The sergeant asked me if I was a member of the Federal Order of Police, as maybe they could help me. I explained to him that I only asked how long I would be in the bars for eight hours straight. I thought it was fair to ask. I only heard from the lieutenant that I was doing a good job.

I recall one evening talking to a couple in a bar about buying a large quantity of drugs. I attempted to call the lieutenant on his pager as instructed. No luck, but he did page me back while I was talking to other potential suspects. He said that he was asleep and couldn't remember what I said. I called him at 10:30 am the next day and told him about buying a large quantity of drugs.

He replied, "The hell with them."

This dealer advised me he would get me whatever I wanted. That ended the chance for a major buy. Remember, I had the lieutenant's police friends following me. They reported that I was not talking to anyone and not doing my job. I had been into three major drug dealers. I had been told to stay away from them all. This is the war on drugs in that county.

HEARINGS AND CHARGES

On October 31 I was subjected to a hearing for charges of gross neglect of duty, failure to obey orders, lack of truthfulness and filing false police reports. The charges and termination were approved by the director and the committee. I was terminated having worked about sixty days or less for that agency. Someone contacted my superior in Alaska for a comment, and he stated in the local newspaper that I was a "highly dedicated police officer." I was recommended for that job by a chief who was also president of the national law group. I could not comprehend how anyone could run that agency by fear and mismanagement and could have concocted these stories in less than sixty days and come up with these phony charges. Ohio is a hire-at-will state, although just cause for dismissal was not necessary in my case, as I did not complete the probationary period.

I was constantly updated on conditions at the agency after October 31 by other agents. In 1987, I had a conversation with an agent I had worked with on the same shift. He told me that the director was doing the same thing to him that had been done to me. He was being charged with dishonesty, failure to obey orders, malfeasance and misfeasance. The director recommended termination for him. He sounded scared and said that he was being followed and was "made" in several bars he was working. He further said that even if he won a lawsuit, he could not stay at the agency. He also said that the leadership consensus was that I was trying to start a union, and that they were trying to get rid of anyone that wanted the union. I never initiated any activity with the union.

The agent also told me that the sergeant said that I was regularly coming to work drunk. The agent told the sergeant that he worked with me, and that I was never drinking before work.

After working eight hours in a bar, one would smell like a barfly. Agents advised me that they were not allowed to have Fraternal Order of Police stickers on their cars, but the director's wife was walking around the garage with a police uniform on and a gold badge. The other agents had requested similar badges but were not allowed to have them.

I met with another ex-undercover agent who told me that the agent I worked with on the same shift had enough information to burn the director at one time but was afraid to do so. Everyone was afraid for their jobs at the agency except the director, the lieutenant, and his wife.

When I left Alaska for this job, I had not been told of this probationary part of the job. I did not even know about it until my first day. I would not have felt secure in the probationary position, as I had the experience and knowledge to conduct myself in any department. I never dreamed the entire probation was meant to have me set up for dismissal.

I was purchasing drugs within weeks of my assignment, fitting into the bars I worked in and was preparing to get to the higher sources of drugs in that county. The administration would not allow me to complete my job. What I don't understand is why that director was ever allowed to continue in that position, which was a do-nothing agency largely because of him. Since Ohio is an at-will state, I would have preferred to have been let go for wearing the wrong colored socks rather than be set up and lied to. After being terminated, I continued to get items of information from ex-agents, current agents and others. I was fully aware of the current agent's fear of their boss and their job. Although they feared for their jobs, one of the agents said all along he would testify on my behalf. I was grateful for that, but he later told me that he was too afraid and would not help me. So much for that!

I was in contact with a lawyer in the county, and I confided in him and asked for his advice regarding my situation. He advised me to talk to a chief of police that he was friends with. I made an appointment with this chief, as I was desperate for help. I asked the chief before that conversation if it would be kept confidential between the two of us. He agreed. The next morning, I was told by an agent that our director received a phone call from the other chief who told him of our conversation.

I taped the conversation about the black book between myself and this agent on March 28, 1988. As mentioned earlier, he had given me the director's wife's memo book. He had seen the book and the prescriptions that she was receiving in suspicious amounts. The amount of the prescriptions we saw was for either 150 or 100 tablets as best as we could make out. We learned that most doctors would only prescribe about thirty a month to a patient. As I mentioned earlier, I could not investigate this matter any further because I had given the book to the Cleveland news reporter. I've never made such a drastic mistake as I did when I gave the female reporter the book instead of a copy. Stupid of me, but I must say the state of mind that I was in was totally alone and desperate to get help from anyone. A lesson I have never forgotten.

Another experienced agent who I became friends with advised me weekly on many matters he observed while in the unit. One I recall was about a major supplier of narcotics during construction of the large plant. The drug dealer had a friend who was also a county employee. This county employee called the director one day and asked him to lay off his friend (name was withheld from agent). The agent was present when the call was received. The investigation on this major drug dealer stopped. Nothing was done. I also understand one of the agents perjured himself on the stand in a drug case, stating that he had observed the transaction when he could not have. He was seen far away from the scene, as witnessed by the agent I was talking to. The suspect was put away for a long time based upon this agent's testimony. The director knew it and did nothing, even though the agent could not identify a picture of the suspect later. Conversations were heard by the agent I was talking to on a weekly basis. The same agent talked about planting cocaine on a suspect, but the director just walked away and did nothing. The director even attempted to set up a sting type operation to nail certain people in the prosecutor's office.

LAST ASSIGNMENT: THE INCIDENT WITH THE HAT

During my last assignment, I was told to wear a hat during my stay in the bar working, supposedly, undercover. It was so obvious to me that the object of the hat was so that the ones hired by the unit's director would be able to follow me or identify me. How I was supposed to act or do a job while in this bar, I will never know. On several incidents, they reported me to be in the bar and then seen to leave the bar at a certain time. Why I was not followed was beyond me, for they may have discovered I was meeting someone to get drug information and possibly set up a buy. A proper surveillance by experienced agents would have uncovered this, but just stated I was not in my assigned bar. I had several witnesses who were going to present this at my hearing, but I was not allowed to use them. Also, these agent friends of the director did not realize that I knew they were cops and had identified one as such. They also did not know that I had friendly witnesses to their actions every night they were in the bar. I also had taped conversations with one of them who came in with his girlfriend. I never saw this information in a report. I was placed in that bar so that they could gather more documentation proving that I was not performing my job.

I was never allowed to do the job that I was hired to do during my short time with this agency, even though I was the only one buying drugs at the time. When I went to get a higher source of drugs, they would assign me to another bar where I would be the one being watched. I never had a chance to succeed during the short time at this agency and was destined for termination by this director from the start. The taped discussion I had with the director's agent and his girlfriend was small talk. He advised me that he cooked for his girlfriend that night. I told him the barmaid was hitting on me. There was not too much going on in the bar other than drunks and loud music. I bought him and his girlfriend a round. His girlfriend was drinking black Russians. I suppose he was also spending narcotics funded money (buy money) from the drug unit to follow me. His girlfriend told me she worked at TRW, a well-known, large company. It was so obvious this cop was told about me by the director, as he tried to get me to talk about illegal poker games and illegal weapons in Alaska. I could play poker, as it was legal. Also, I owned an automatic weapon that was legal, as I had an ATF stamp.

I always questioned the director's previous department employees working for him. How did he account for the money he was paying them when the agency was by funded by taxpayers? My conversation with this person continued about hunting with fifty-eight caliber Hawkens rifles. I just played the game but often wanted to punch one or two of them, as I was disgusted with the whole situation. I sat there with this guy, all the time my stomach was churning. Why did I not see his report in the file about these evening surveillances? By the way, since leaving this agency, I have not been sick since the time I worked for them. I'm still actively working and have nothing seriously wrong with me.

During my life I believe I was an honest person and never found a reason to lie to anyone. Most people that know me will attest to this fact. I remember one time, I was about thirty years old and working as an assistant store manager. It was near Christmas time. I walked into the store, as I was returning for lunch, and discovered an envelope on the store floor. I opened the envelope and discovered $300 inside. I went to the store's office and noticed an elderly lady walking in the store, crying her heart out. I asked her what the matter was. She told me that she lost her husband's money that was to be for their Christmas. She told me of the current amount of money, and I returned the money to her. Another time, when I owned the convenience store, my wife and I were making a drop-off deposit at the bank. Nearby I discovered large amounts of money just blowing in the wind, loosely getting caught in the bushes. I started to scoop the money up and put it in my pocket, as it was everywhere. The bank was not open yet; it was in the early daylight hours. If I remember correctly, we found about $1600 to $2000. When the bank opened, I went to the bank and turned it in. It was also near Christmas when I found the money. The bank held onto the money for the required days and no one reported the money missing. We were given back the money. Both times I could've used the money and not said anything to anyone. I did the right thing because this was how I was raised. I have never compromised my integrity by stealing anything from anybody.

I always wished I could have taken a polygraph regarding my experience in the narcotics unit and the people in the administration I was dealing with. Obviously, this never happened, as I was not allowed to defend myself in the ire at-will state of Ohio. There is nothing in this writing and statements I've made that is untrue. As I have documented, most of this in my personal notes and recordings. I would have volunteered at any time to take a polygraph but never got the chance.

TWO LETTERS OF ENDORSEMENT

For reference purposes, and to show what a good investigator I had been in Alaska, please read the following endorsement written by my former supervisor of the Metro Drug Unit in Alaska:

"I directed Karl to make inquiry using a cover story on those occasions. Karl worked out very well. He was never burned on any surveillance nor any of us field contacts with informants. This may not sound unusual in a large community but in our closed environment, I feel his success is indicative of his natural talent for undercover work. As his supervisor, I would rate Karl's work as above average. He was able to motivate informants, keep track of money properly and handle evidence and keep up his workload during this time with the Metro Drug Unit. He got

along with his fellow officers and me as a supervisor in a very congenial fashion. We had a lot of fun and got a lot of work done. I would not hesitate to hire him back as an undercover agent. I would qualify that by saying that he would, of course, must be assigned to a community other than the one in which he lived and worked so long as a uniformed officer. I feel his success is indicative of his natural talent for undercover work. Karl's strength is in his ability to think quickly on his feet. He is also able to adjust his mannerism to fit any situation. Karl has several life's experiences that will serve him in good state in formulating cover stories as well as acting out the parts necessary to make such stories believable. I believe him to be a dedicated police officer who would do you a very good job. Karl had worked for me for approximately eight months."

I add the following letter of commendation from my previous employer to show the reader that my previous record of professionalism belies what has been said by my current management.

"I would like to recommend Corporal Karl R. Lewkowski receive a letter of commendation for his actions in regard to the arrest of William and Audrey Lawrence on 7/15/85. After reviewing the case and talking with numerous witnesses, I feel Corporal Lewkowski handled himself in a professional manner, reflecting favorably upon the Juneau Police Department.

The facts of the case were as follows:

On 7/15/85, at 1941 hours, the Juneau Police department received a complaint of a domestic disturbance at the downtown ferry terminal. The complainant also stated that a male subject was intoxicated and had been driving.

Upon Corporal Lewkowski's arrival at the ferry terminal, he was confronted by William and Audrey Lawrence. He was verbally abused by the Lawrences, more so however by William Lawrence. William Lawrence was ranting and raving and was very uncooperative. William Lawrence was cursing at Corporal Lewkowski, stating things like "fuck you" and "asshole". This was repeated numerous times. William Lawrence would get right up next to Corporal Lewkowski's face as he was yelling and cussing at him. William Lawrence was being abusive toward Corporal Lewkowski as he was throwing his license and registration at Corporal Lewkowsi and being quite obnoxious. When Lawrence was also making threatening gestures toward Corporal Lewkowski Lawrence would clench his fists and make movements toward Corporal Lewkowski. Corporal Lewkowski, knowing that an arrest was imminent, radioed for backup before proceeding to make the physical arrest on William Lawrence. Knowing that William Lawrence was an ex professional boxer, Corporal Lewkowski knew that he would have to hurt William Lawrence if he attempted the arrest by himself.

There were probably at least fifty to one hundred people in the immediate vicinity while all this was taking place. Corporal Lewkowski "swallowed his pride" and "maintained his cool" in the face of this adversity. Numerous witnesses stated they felt Corporal Lewkowski did a very fine job in regard to the Lawrence arrest. They stated that he acted with an extreme amount of restraint in dealing with William Lawrence. At no time did any witness observe Corporal Lewkowski demonstrate and behavior or mannerisms that could be construed as aggressive. They in fact stated that Corporal Lewkowski acted in a very non-violent and professional manner. Some witnesses went so far as to say that even after the arrest was effected, Corporal Lewkowski showed no emotion or animosity toward the Lawrences. They stated that he was very "matter of fact" and very "businesslike".

There is no doubt in my mind that with Corporal Lewkowski's strength, size, expertise in the martial arts and his proficiency with the Tonfa, he could have taken William Lawrence by himself. Corporal Lewkowski however called for and waited for backup before arresting William Lawrence even though he was taking much verbal abuse. Then, when effecting the arrest on Lawrence Williams, Corporal Lewkowski only used that force which was necessary. Corporal Lewkowski kept a calm, cool, professional bearing, resulting in numerous witnesses complimenting the way in which he handled himself.

Signed: Michael S. Gelston. Chief of Police

IN SUMMARY

We had returned to Ohio where I was eager to start my new career with a county drug unit. I came highly recommended for the position coming from an effective drug unit in Alaska. I had no idea that I was set up for failure before I even started. The agency was poorly managed, highly political, and overseen by a dysfunctional board of directors. Agent morale was disastrously low, so the unit's effectiveness was minimal. Here I arrive from Alaska thinking that I was hired to help the agency go after higher levels of the drug gang hierarchy, but I soon learned that leadership in the agency did not trust me; they thought that I was hired by their political enemies to displace them. Ultimately, I was fired after just a short time there.

It would be inappropriate for me to write or discuss anything about the unit since I left. I wrote from my experience only. It has been thirty-four years since I was terminated from the agency. I have no idea how they are doing today, nor do I know who is on the board. I will not speak or write anything negative about the agents or the person running the unit. It was exceedingly difficult for me to have to relive the events that I have about written in this book. In my next occupation, Private Investigations, I would be my own boss and take my past experiences with me and hopefully learn from them.

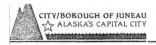

August 6, 1985

TO: Michael S. Gelston
         Chief of Police

FROM: Steven S. Kalwara
         Sergeant of Police

SUBJECT: Letter of Commendation

I would like to recommend Corporal Karl R. Lewkowski receive a letter of commendation for his actions in regards to the arrest of William and Audrey LAWRENCE on 7/15/85. After reviewing the case and talking with numerous witnesses, I feel Corporal Lewkowski handled himself in a professional manner, reflecting favorably upon the Juneau Police Department.

The facts of the case were as follows:

> On 7/15/85, at 1941 hours, the Juneau Police Department received a complaint of a domestic disturbance at the downtown ferry terminal. The complainant also stated that a male subject was intoxicated and had been driving.

> Upon Corporal Lewkowski's arrival at the ferry terminal, he was confronted by William and Audrey LAWRENCE. He was verbally abused by the LAWRENCES, more so however by William LAWRENCE. William LAWRENCE was ranting and raving and was very uncooperative. William LAWRENCE was cursing at Corporal Lewkowski, stating things like "fuck you" and "asshole". This was repeated numerous times. William LAWRENCE would get right up next to Corporal Lewkowski's face as he was yelling and cussing at him. William LAWRENCE was being abusive towards Corporal Lewkowski as he was throwing his license and registration at Corporal Lewkowski and being quite obnoxious. When LAWRENCE was also making threatening gestures towards Corporal Lewkowski, LAWRENCE would clench his fists and make movements toward Corporal Lewkowski.

> Corporal Lewkowski, knowing that an arrest was imminent, radioed for backup before proceeding to make the physical arrest on William LAWRENCE. Knowing that William LAWRENCE was an ex-professional boxer, Corporal Lewkowski knew that he would most likely have to hurt William LAWRENCE if he attempted the arrest by himself.

> There were probably at least 50 to 100 people in the immediate vicinity while all this was taking place. Corporal Lewkowski "swallowed his pride" and "maintained his cool" in the face of this adversity. Numerous witnesses stated they felt Corporal Lewkowski did a very fine job in regards to the LAWRENCE arrest. They stated that he acted with an extreme amount of restraint in dealing with William LAWRENCE. At no time did any witness observe Corporal Lewkowski demonstrate any behavior or mannerisms that could be construed as aggressive. They in fact stated that Corporal Lewkowski acted in a very non-violent and professional manner. Some witnesses went as far as to say that even after the arrest was effected, Corporal Lewkowski showed no emotion or animosity towards the LAWRENCES. They stated that he was very "matter of fact" and very "businesslike".

There is no doubt in my mind that with Corporal Lewkowski's strength, size, expertise in the martial arts and his proficiency with the Tonfa, he could have "taken" William LAWRENCE by himself. Corporal Lewkowski however called for and waited for backup before arresting William LAWRENCE even though he was taking much verbal abuse. Then, when effecting the arrest on William LAWRENCE, Corporal Lewkowski only used that force which was necessary. Corporal Lewkowski kept a calm, cool, professional bearing, resulting in numerous witnesses complimenting the way in which he handled himself.

SSK/plh

CHAPTER EIGHT

PRIVATE INVESTIGATOR

M Y LIFE AFTER LEAVING THE narcotics agency was in disarray. I was at the lowest point I can ever remember in my life. It seemed that I had lost everything that I have ever worked for. I was angry, frustrated, and disappointed in the people who recruited me for the agent's job. I have always been in control of my life and knew exactly what I was going to do. My wife, Toni, always stood by my side. If not for her, I may not have pursued my career as a private investigator. Toni encouraged me to take the test and start my own business. Thank God for her help, as I sure needed it.

After thinking about it, I took the state test for a "Class A" private investigator's license, scoring 92 percent. The Class A granted me authority to operate as a PI and/or Private Security. I named my new business Argus Investigations Agency. I started the business with nothing more than an 800 number, business cards, and a brochure.

While my new business was slowly developing, I took a job with a small local police department. I attended the Ohio police training academy at Lakeland College for a short mandatory program on domestic violence. I was then able to get certified as a police officer in Ohio.

I am grateful that my new chief hired me, even though I had been terminated from the drug unit. He believed in me and knew my situation. At one time, while in his office, a phone call came in from one of the county officials wanting to know why the chief had hired me. The chief put the phone on speaker so I could listen. He ably defended his hiring of me to this official. I had the utmost respect for him and knew him to be an honest, honorable person.

Another chief who also knew what transpired at the drug unit also stuck by me, and we became close friends. This was Chief Thomas Fracci, another honorable police professional and a great friend. We are still close friends now; I help care for Tom, as he is ninety-three years old. More about him later in my story. Tom also backed me up when I was nominated to join the Fraternal Order of Police (FOP) in Lake County.

I resigned from the local PD after about a year or so, as my new business now needed me full time.

ARGUS INVESTIGATION AGENCY

I was now a full-time private investigator working out of my home office. My wife, Toni, was my "Chief of Staff" in our one-person office. She did all the office work, without which we would not have made it. We had a policy of always answering the phone—no answering machines allowed! We followed this policy seven days a week and twenty-four hours a day. We gained many clients with this simple strategy. Clients would always comment that we were not like the other guys! After-hours calls almost always resulted in a new case. Clients were uncomfortable leaving messages, so always answering their calls made a difference.

I looked like a cop with my refrigerator build and gray fringe of short-cut hair. Although standing only 5'6, I was physically capable of handling myself and looked it. My investigative credentials were solid. The challenge now was to build Argus Investigations a reputation for integrity and effectiveness; finding clients was my priority. The Yellow Pages was the go-to place for first time PI clients back then, so Argus was listed up there with Acme, Ace, and all the other As. We also sent out brochures to likely sources of business, such as law firms.

One source of business during startup was workers' compensation cases.

WORKERS' COMPENSATION INVESTIGATIONS

Workers' compensation cases became a steady source of work once I got into the system. These cases came from insurers who were being suckered into paying large sums of money to employees who were injured on the job and could no longer work. A large percentage of these injured parties were phonies looking to game the system.

Workers compensation insurance protects employees who are hurt on the job. This valued employee benefit pays for medical expenses, lost wages and other expenses while a worker heals. Most employers and their workers are honest. However, a small number scam this coverage for personal profit, but the damage they cause is enormous. Workers' comp fraud is a large crime in America today. Tens of billions of dollars in false claims and unpaid premiums are stolen every year. Scams are forcing premiums higher—draining business profits and costing honest workers their pay and jobs. And guess what—you pay higher prices at the cash register. The large costs of fraud get passed onto all consumers.

Workers' comp cases usually meant surveilling the suspect to catch them in an act that belied their reported injury. Sometimes an investigator must get creative in order to capture the miscreant performing tasks that belied injury.

THE HORSEWOMAN

One such case involved a woman who claimed that her back injury limited her ability to work. I arrived at her residence to find that she lived in the country at what appeared to be a small horse ranch. A long dirt driveway surrounded by trees and foliage would prevent me from surveilling the suspect at home. Following her whenever she left the property would be the only way to have any chance at watching her activity. I was not excited by that method of discovery, as it was very time consuming and not usually fruitful. Shopping or going to the hair salon were not as credible as working out in the yard chopping firewood!

I noticed a sign near her mailbox that said horse riding lessons were available here and gave a phone number. I went back to the office and decided to try another tactic. I dialed the number I saw on the sign, and a woman answered the phone. I asked her about riding lessons for my young granddaughter who just loved horses. Could I schedule a time to bring her out to see if riding lessons would be something she would enjoy? We made an appointment for an "introductory" ride for later that same week.

I arrived at the farm with my excited granddaughter. We parked by the house and found our suspect out by the barn. We exchanged pleasantries while our host led a horse out of its stall. Now, being the doting grandpa that I was, I prepared to take a movie of my granddaughter's first equestrian experience. I pointed my camera while my suspect reached down and swung a heavy saddle onto the horse, followed a few minutes later by my granddaughter. So much for the back injury. My evidence should be enough to close this case. The following are my case notes from this case. The reader can see that a PI must sometimes use imagination to gather evidence.

I was requested by MC, an attorney with the firm of B&T, to conduct a two-day surveillance upon MPS, at horse farm, located at Concord, Ohio. I was given a brief description of the plaintiff, MPS, and was advised that "MPS" was claiming injuries to her right arm, neck, and back.

HORSEWOMAN CASE NOTES:

On 5-9-94, I conducted a preliminary check of the farm. Construction is in progress near the farm, as crews are repairing the bridge over State

Route 44. One-way traffic is in progress during the construction period and after work hours. The property to the west of the farm abuts the Route 44 highway, which runs north and south. North of the house and barns is an open area that joins the woods and trails. South of the house and barns is the roadway under construction. East of the house and barns is a field and wooded area. Surveillance, without being on the property and inside the horse barns, to personally observe MPS, is almost impossible. The woods are also posted "no trespassing."

On 5-13-94, I placed a call to the farm, and was advised by MPS's mother that MPS is "on the trail now and giving lessons and stuff." The time of the call was 10:45 am. MPS's mother advised me that MPS would be on the trail to 11:30 am and back out at twelve pm and would return at about 2:30 pm. I was also advised that we cannot look around the farm, as the thoroughbred horses are "kind of touchy." MPS's mother further advised me that lessons are $16 for a 1/2 hr lesson.

I telephoned the law offices of B&T to request permission to have horse lessons paid for as part of the expenses relating to this case. I was given the go ahead by the secretary.

I drove back to the farm to pick up a release form, as requested by MPS's mother, prior to beginning the horse lessons. I had the release forms signed and returned to the farm. Back at the farm, I observed MPS in a horse barn wearing Levis, a sweatshirt, and a blue bandanna around her head. MPS was alone in a stall with a horse. I had approached her just as she had placed a saddle on the horse and was tightening the straps around the hors, using her right hand and arm quite vigorously. MPS advised me that we could return to the farm at six pm for the first lesson. I paid MPS $52.50 for three 1/2 hr lessons.

At six pm, upon entry to the horse barn, I observed a western saddle on the ground in front of the horse stable. I observed MPS bend over and pick up the saddle, carry it into the stall area, and place it upon the horses back. The saddle used on the first lesson was a western saddle, weighing approximately twelve pounds. I later learned that one has to lift the saddle on to the horses' back—not just throw it onto the back of the horse. This action of lifting the saddle and setting it on the back of the horse requires a moderate amount of strength. I believe MPS is right handed, as I observed her earlier in the day tightening the straps around a horse, and now at 6:02 pm she is doing the same thing to this horse. At 6:10 pm, inside the arena area, MPS is observed grabbing the reins of the horse and running alongside the horse. MPS is holding the reins with her right hand. At 6:15 pm, MPS is observed tightening the stirrups on the horse and at 6:20 pm using her right arm. At 6:21 pm MPS is running alongside the horse as she instructs the student. At 6:34 pm MPS is observed mounting the horse and getting off the horse as she demonstrates the correct method. At 6:35 pm MPS is observed loosening the saddle on the horse. The lesson lasted approximately 1/2 hr.

The second lesson was scheduled for 9:30 am on 5-14-94. Upon arrival at the farm, another young lady was assigned to give the second lesson. MPS was in process of giving haircuts to the horses, also stating to me that she had to feed the horses. The implement to cut the horsehair was in MPS's right hand, and a brush was in her left hand. MPS was observed lifting an English saddle from a rack and handing it to the other instructor.

On May 15, 1994, I arrived at the farm at approximately 9:20 am to begin the third lesson. MPS was to be the instructor today. I observed MPS carry a saddle from the saddle room, carry it to the stall, and set it on the ground. At 9:26 am MPS placed the saddle on the back of the horse and tightened the straps with her right hand. MPS had brushed the horse prior to placing the saddled on its back. In the arena area, MPS tightened the stirrups on the saddle twice during the lesson. Prior to entering the arena, MPS swung open the metal gate at the entrance and removed two wooden slats at the entrance to the arena, lifting them and placing them on the ground. At the end of the lesson, MPS is handed the saddle, which she grasped with her left hand. I later learned that an English saddle weighs about eight to ten pounds without stirrups.

LYING EMPLOYEE

A client, whom I will refer to as GL, requested that I investigate an employee, whom I will call MM, who would be in the Columbus area the weekend of March 25th, 1994. MM had submitted a claim to GL that he, MM, had injured his back while in the employment of GL. GL provided me with the name of the hotel where MM and other friends of his would be staying. To give my reader the feel for this kind of investigation, I include my notes and log entries of this case as follows:

On Friday March 25th, 1994, I stayed at the Holiday Inn in Worthington, Columbus area, where MM was registered. I drove to several places GL had advised me the group may be located. I made contact with JB and MM in the hotel lobby of the Holiday Inn at approximately five pm. GL had given me a description of MM and JB prior to my arrival in Columbus. I observe MM and JB (a friend of MM) sitting in the hotel lounge with an attractive female sitting with them.

I observed the waiter deliver an order of shrimp cocktail to their table. My back was to the three of them, and I did not observe MM and the female leave the bar—but they had left. I did observe JB at the hotel bar as he ordered a bottle of wine, a pitcher of long island iced tea, and four glasses. I spoke to JB briefly and asked him who the female was. He indicated to me the female was with MM. JB indicated to me that MM was quite the lady's man. JB was quite intoxicated when I observed him in the bar. I offered to help him carry the drinks to his room, as I told him I was also going to my room. I carried the pitcher of long island iced tea to room #417.

In Room #417 I observed one male in each of the two beds. The shower was running in the bathroom, and whoever was in the bathroom closed the door as I entered the room. I put the pitcher on the table and left. JB had advised me the group he was with would be at a bar called Sylvia's Back Door. The bar is located by the Worthington Mall.

At 9:30 pm, 3-25-94, I observe JB in Sylvia's Bar. He is obviously very intoxicated, as he advised me they would not serve him any more beer. I did not see MM or any of the other group of guys until 10:15 pm. MM was wearing a white shirt buttoned to the collar with what appeared to be small print or dots on the shirt—he was wearing dark pants. I observe MM fast dancing with a tall blond female. He did not appear to have anything wrong with his back. MM was moving and twisting his upper and lower body while dancing. Prior to dancing with this female, I observed MM standing near the dance floor dancing to the music by himself, twisting and turning his upper body and moving his legs to the music. He did not appear to have any type of problem moving to the music. At 11:45 pm I observe the same female that was with MM at the Holiday Inn bar earlier in the day. She was wearing a red top and dark bottom outfit. It was obvious to me the female was with MM, as he stayed close to her during my observations. At 12:45 pm I observe MM dancing with this female to a fairly fast musical beat. He did not appear to have any back problems during the time I observed him at Sylvia's Back Door.

At 12:45 am I leave the bar in an attempt to photograph MM leaving the bar. I observe MM and three other guys with him enter the Jeep Cherokee belonging to JB. MM is driving the Cherokee. I could not see when the female left the bar. At 2:15 am I observe the Cherokee in

front of the Holiday Inn with guys exiting the vehicle. I also observe the female driving an '88 Ford two door, Ohio license NGW 289. I observe one of MM's friends exit the vehicle that the female was driving. I could not see where the female parked, but her vehicle, however, I did observe MM leave the Holiday Inn parking lot with the female in the passenger seat. They drive to a United Dairy Farmers store on Worthington Woods

Road, then I observe them drive to a Kroger store and back to the United Dairy store again. I leave them at the United Dairy store at 2:35 am and return to the Holiday Inn.

At 2:43 am I observe the Cherokee return to the Holiday Inn. I was stopped by the security guard on duty and could not determine if the female returned to MM's room with him or left her vehicle. The 1988 Ford two door is registered to DW, 835 Pineway Drive, Worthington Ohio.

On Saturday, 3-26-94, at 8:30 am, I awoke to see if I could locate the 1988 Ford in the parking lot—I did not see it. The Cherokee was backed into a handicapped parking spot. I observed a white Lexus KWS 494, a Pontiac four door, blue, Ohio license VHE 855 with Ashtabula plates. A red Camry VWY 236 was parked next to the blue Pontiac with a Lake County tag.

At eight pm I drive to Sylvia's Back Door. I observed the group of guys with JB arrive at the bar. I recall about seven guys in this group from Ashtabula arrive at approximately 10:15 pm. It was approximately eleven pm when I observe MM wearing a white shirt buttoned to the collar and white/black shoes. MM was near the dance floor keeping beat to the music. (I recall my back hurting both night, as as I was on my feet most of the time. I finally sat at a table Friday night.) I did not recall MM ever standing still for any length of time, nor did I see him sitting down. It appeared to me that MM arrived at Sylvia's with a fairly large female (175#) or so. The bar was not as busy as it was on Friday, and the group left very quickly at 12:06 am.

I was running to my car as it was raining—and could observe the rest of their group running toward their vehicles. Four or five guys got into the white Lexus. I believe MM, and possibly two females, entered a red car that was in front of the Lexus. Due to the rain, and where they both were parked, I had a difficult time seeing what was happening. I followed the white Lexus. The red car was in front of the Lexus driving to Rt. 270 west. I could not see the license plate of the red vehicle. At 12:15 am we were in a downpour. I observe both vehicles drive into a parking lot to a nightclub called Dazzler's.

I observe the white Lexus park in the lot but could not see where the red vehicle parked.

It was approximately 12:20 am when we arrived at Dazzlers. At 01:33 am the group in the Lexus left the bar. I did not see MM leave the bar. I went in the bar to see if I could observe him or the females he was with, but I could not locate him or the vehicle he arrived in.

I returned to Sylvia's bar at two am. I observe another Ashtabula license plate VOB 216, a white Dodge Colt in the parking lot. On Sunday morning, 3-27-94, I observed the Lincoln Town car PHP 685 at the Holiday Inn parking lot. This was the first time I observed this car.

My notes ended at this point, but my surveillance notes give you an idea of how complicated things can get when doing this kind of surveillance.

SURVEILLANCE

Surveillance is one of the basic elements of a PI's tool kit. Most cases that a PI works require surveillance of some type while some cases are entirely surveillance. A client may just want someone followed to see where they go and what they do. Another client might want photographic or other evidence gathered on each contact. Surveillance can be very basic or extremely complex, requiring more than one person or vehicle.

I, and one of my investigators, flew to New York for foot surveillance on a female. I was advised the female was a former informant for another government agency outside of the United States. I was assigned to just monitor her activities and photograph any associates she would be with. We were doing quite well on the foot surveillance when, one afternoon, the female left the building and hailed a cab. Having no vehicle nearby, I saw many yellow cabs coming toward us and flagged one down. I ordered the driver to, "Follow that car!"

He turned around and, in a Middle Eastern accent, replied to me, "I no do that."

I told him that I would double his salary for the day. He still would not do what I asked. Luckily, we had an idea where the subject was going and found her later. That was the only time we had to get in the car. I asked other cab drivers if they would have honored my request, and they all stated they would. At the end of the surveillance, we presented the client with a report. He was satisfied with the job we had completed for him.

As he was a jeweler, my client called me after the case was completed and was going to send me a gift of some sort. I told him that he didn't have to do that, and I don't normally wear jewelry, but he sent me three bracelets through the mail to my office. So, I picked out one bracelet, sent the other two back, and thanked him for the gift.

The following article from the News Herald was written after the reporter went out on a case with me. The reporter wanted to see what it was really like to be a private investigator versus what we see on TV. I had to get a client to agree to this, and, when I had one, I called the reporter and invited him to our pre-case conference at my home office. The meeting was held at Argus' headquarters—my home. Attending were my wife Toni and my sometimes assistant, my daughter Connie. The case was a typical divorce case where the client wanted evidence of infidelity by a spouse. The mission was to gather the evidence by surveillance.

The reporter learned three things about a PI's typical surveillance.

1. It is tedious and requires patience and the ability to maintain vigilant while sitting in a vehicle for hours.

2. Tailing a suspect in traffic without getting burned can be exceedingly difficult and complex.

3. Sometimes a PI must be creative to complete the task and acquire actual evidence. The evidence gathered in this case were two photos of the spouse and her lover.

The reporter starts out with a fictitious account of his expectations of a TV-type private investigator.

THE REPORTER RIDES ALONG

The Case of a Real-Life Detective
As Written by Mark D. Somerson in the
News-Herald Aug. 19, 1990

Chapter One

The evening air was as cool as a breeze through a morgue, but I could sense that I was in for a hot night. I looked out my apartment window past the glow of neon and watched the sun quickly set behind the grey of the city—it was time to go.

As I drove into Willoughby to meet my partner, I thought about the night—somewhere out there—out in those dingy streets, there was someone up to no good, and it was up to us to catch 'em in the act.

I walked into our dimly lit office and took a seat. I tossed my hat onto my partner's desk and asked him for the skinny. "Some palooka thinks his wife is two-timing him on the sly and wants proof," he said without looking up from the ash tray he was studying.

No sweat, I thought to myself as I lit a cigarette. A good flatfoot could handle a divorce case in his sleep.

My partner signaled it was time to hit the pavement—after all, we couldn't collect any greenbacks until we had the goods on the skirt and her boyfriend.

We got into his car and drove to an apartment complex in the city where our client and his wife lived. We spotted the wife's wheels and settled in for the wait. In this racket, a lot of time is spent waiting—waiting and drinking cups of cold java trying to keep your peepers on the right person.

After what seemed like an eternity, the dame stepped out of a doorway and into the cold light of the moon. She quickly looked around the lot before getting in her car—she was nervous. In fact, she was shaking like a belly dancer on hot coals.

She started her engine and pulled out. As she drove past us, we started the car and took our place behind her on the street. From now on it was follow the leader, and I had a gut feeling that wherever this dame was leading us, it was someplace I would rather not be.

My partner looked over at me and winked—he looked calm, but I knew he felt that same feeling I just did . . . there was danger down the road, and we were driving into it wheels first . . .

Well, that is how I envisioned it anyway. I guess a steady diet of Dashiel Hammett books and Humphrey Bogart movies can do that to a reporter who gets the chance to go out on a stakeout with a private investigator.

But as fast as my imagination could provide a night of 1940s adventure, Karl Lewkowski's calculated brand of detecting brought me back to 1990s reality. Lewkowski, a private eye since 1987, owns Argus Investigations Agency in Willoughby. I contacted him about two months ago and told him I was interested in comparing day-to-day detective work to what television and the silver screen offer. I even went so far as to ask him if I could tag along with him on a case.

To my surprise the former Juneau, Alaska, police officer and narcotics agent said it was all right with him as long as it was cleared with his clients. A few weeks ago, he called me with the good news—a client said it didn't matter if I wrote about his case.

I armed myself with a notebook and pen that Saturday night and sped over to the private investigator's office. At the last minute, I decided to ditch the trench coat—I'm glad I did. When I got there. Lewkowski, his wife Toni, and their daughter Connie were discussing the case in their apartment, which also serves as their office.

Lewkowski, fifty, told me his daughter was going out with us that night— he said in his racket, an extra pair of eyes is almost always needed. At 7:45, he said it was time to go, so we walked out to the parking lot and got into his new Toyota. She got into another small model car, and we were on our way.

As we drove down Lost Nations Road, Lewkowski told me about the case—a man suspected his wife was cheating on him and wanted proof.

For the next six hours, Lewkowski and his daughter systematically dashed every preconceived notion I had concerning private investigators and stakeouts. I thought I did my homework by watching the Maltese Falcon and Magnum P.I. reruns, but fiction is just that, fiction.

What really goes on is waiting—a whole lot of waiting. Sure, there's a car chase now and then, but the suspect rarely knows he or she is being followed.

There's also a lot of thinking involved. Solving a case isn't as simple as firing a gun now and then and kissing the beautiful woman until someone confesses right before the commercial. Uncovering a pattern and determining the next move is protocol, protecting your cover is paramount.

During the course of the evening, Lewkowski and his daughter discovered why their client's wife was visiting a Lake County apartment complex and who she was seeing. It wasn't terribly exciting, but it did prove interesting.

As we followed the woman from her apartment complex to the other, I learned something about shadowing a suspect—it's not easy. Driving on a busy freeway is difficult enough, but try doing it while talking on the radio and attempting to maintain invisibility.

Once we got to the other apartment complex, we ran into a slight problem—there was a security gate equipped with a guard.

Lewkowski flashed his badge to the guard, and we went in.

"He didn't have to let me in, you know," he said as we passed the gate. "I'm going to have to buy him a six-pack or something once we leave."

Although we lost some time at the security gate, we found our suspect's car empty and parked. We eased into a spot nearby and settled in for another wait.

What followed was a bit confusing but can best be described as a wild goose chase. We saw a woman who fit our suspect's description get into a pickup truck and leave the complex with two men.

Lewkowski said he had to take the chance and follow in case it was her. For the next forty minutes we tailed that pickup truck all over the east side of Cleveland.

And I learned another lesson: traffic lights seldom wait for private detectives. To put it bluntly, we ran a few lights that sported shades of red to keep an eye on the truck.

It turns out this woman was not our suspect, but Lewkowski said sometimes a private investigator has to take chances. We headed back to the apartment complex and settled in for another wait.

Meanwhile, in between calls to his client, Lewkowski got his wife on the phone to call the Bureau of Motor Vehicles in Columbus to check on the "other man." The client had clued us into his name and a college address.

We soon got a call back that proved interesting—this man's car was registered to the apartment complex we were parked in. We took a quick drive through the lot, but his car wasn't there.

We did check the registry in the apartment building the woman's car was parked near, and the man's name was there. Things were starting to fall into place.

"Now all we have to do is wait for the two to come back from wherever they are," Lewkowski said with a smile. "The case is pretty much solved."

And we did wait—about another two hours before the suspect and the man drove up in his car. At 1:30 am, Lewkowski snapped a few pictures of the two together. We were done.

Sure. There were no gun fights, and fine, we didn't break into any offices and make off with any top-secret information, but we did solve the case. It might not have been the stuff dime store novels are made of, but Lewkowski P.I. took care of business.

THE LONG RIDE

I was once given a surveillance case that started in downtown Cleveland. I had no idea where the target would end up, but I did anticipate being home that night. The client wanted to know where the target went and to obtain an address where he stopped. That was the assignment, and the client was clear that I was to do whatever it took. I had a PI intern with me—a young man who wanted to learn the business. I often needed some help with a case so decided to see how this guy might fit in. He was a big guy and physically intimidating. He could be useful in many circumstances.

Our plan was to stake out the target's office in downtown Cleveland and follow him when he left. We had planned to change vehicles to a rental prior to beginning our surveillance. I was driving my five series BMW and was expecting a rental car to be delivered at 7:30 am. The rental car was not only late, but the object of my surveillance left earlier than we were told to expect. We had no choice but to follow in the BMW instead of a car with less gas consumption.

We followed the target to Interstate Highway 71 where he turned south. Our orders were to follow no matter what. The client never warned us that we might be in for a long trip! I had a full tank of gas, a companion, and the feeling that we might be in for a long one.

We continued south through Ohio, Kentucky, and almost into Tennessee when I absolutely had to stop for gas. The tank was getting dangerously low, so I sped past our target and exited the freeway at the next exit. I sped to the nearest gas station, fueled my vehicle to capacity, and got back on the freeway heading south. As I was entering the freeway, the target vehicle was right in front of us. It was perfect timing. What luck! When our target finally stopped for gas, we were able to top off again without getting burned.

We continued driving south when I had to relieve myself, but we could not stop. My intern steered the vehicle from the right seat as I emptied my bladder into my relief bottle while operating the gas pedal. We were laughing quite hard by then, but what else could I do? I could not lose the suspect vehicle. The surveillance ended after fifteen hours and a thousand miles somewhat north of New Orleans. It was dark when the subject pulled into a driveway. We noted the mailbox with the address turned around and drove back home. We took turns sleeping on the way back.

I was told by a good source that if federal agents had been tasked with this case, they would have used five cars and an aircraft on this job, and that is with a GPS attached to the target vehicle.

INFIDELITY CASE

I never imagined this one when I went into the PI business! A call came in one morning from what sounded like an older gentleman. He would not discuss his situation on the phone, so we agreed to meet at a coffee shop near his home. We met at the shop and sat down with some coffee. He looked to be in his early sixties. It was early morning, yet he wore a jacket and tie and appeared to be very rational. He told me that he wanted me to check up on his wife who he suspected of "fooling around." He then handed me a small bag in which he claimed was a pair of his wife's panties. Now, I struggled to keep a straight face as he asked that I have the panties "tested" for evidence. He also wanted me to follow her for a day or so to find out where her assignations were taking place. I took the case, as he seemed sincere and credible. We settled on the details, and I planned to start surveillance the following day.

In the meantime, I would find a lab where I could have the garment analyzed for forensic evidence. I found a lab that could perform this service, so sent them the garment.

The next morning, I started surveillance by parking close by my client's house while waiting for the old gentleman's randy wife to leave home. For two days I followed her until she returned home. The nice-looking lady shopped, went to the hairdresser, and even visited a church. I was convinced that she was as innocent as could be.

I contacted my client and told him what I had observed, and that I did not want to keep taking his money. I also told him the results I had gotten back from the lab. He could rest easy, as there was no evidence that the nice lady was being unfaithful.

I was talking with my brother who lives in Anchorage and described my latest case. He laughed and said that maybe this was a new business opportunity. He said that I should consider establishing "panty kiosks" in malls where clients could drop off garments for analysis! We had a good laugh but discarded that idea.

FIRST "BURN"

I recall a surveillance case where I was "burned" within minutes of entering the upscale neighborhood where I was going to work. Within a minute of slowly passing my target's house, I saw a door open and a person staring at my vehicle, which was a '94 BMW. As I circled the neighborhood to leave, a car began following me out of the neighborhood. I was quite shocked to have been burned so quickly and immediately thought something was terribly wrong. It was toward evening and getting dark outside. I went north on a highway heading toward Geauga County. I was traveling at a high rate of speed with the subject close to my vehicle. There was not much traffic, so I could not lose the guy.

I was eventually pulled over by a local police officer who asked for my identification. (I later learned the man had called a police department and advised them of the chase.) I explained to the officer who I was and what I was doing. I was not cited for anything.

I have done thousands of hours of surveillance and was quite shocked the way I was burned so quickly. I called a friend of mine the next morning and told him of my experience. He called me later in the day and told me what had happened. The neighborhood where I was working was on high alert for a possible child predator. That's why the neighborhood watch person followed me from the neighborhood. I later learned the man had called a police department and advised them of the chase. I was impressed with the way the neighborhood had organized to protect their community!

SERVING PAPERS

I recall the first papers that I had served as a private investigator was to be served upon a lawyer in the Cleveland area. I left my office to serve the papers on this person whose office was in a downtown Cleveland building. I approached the office door and discovered that the door was locked, but I heard a man talking on the phone. From the conversation, I could hear it was the person I was to serve the papers on. I awaited nearby to spot the individual leaving his office. It was not long before I saw the door handle moving as if the subject was going to leave. I approached the door and opened it, and the subject was standing directly in front of me when I handed him the necessary paperwork. I turned and left the building, returned to my vehicle, and was driving eastbound about ten minutes after serving the paper when the attorney that hired me called and said to me that the subject in question shot himself. I felt very disturbed by this, but if it weren't me, it would have been somebody else serving him papers.

RUNNING THE RED LIGHTS

This case was not the first time that I had contact with the police while working a case. On another surveillance I was stopped by the local police, who advised me that I had driven through several red lights. I showed the proper identification to the officer, and he asked me if I was working; I said that I was. He was very polite and understanding and made me aware that he saw me look both ways before proceeding through the lights. I thanked him for his courtesy and continued my surveillance as I (luckily) caught up with my target vehicle.

Normally when we conduct a surveillance, we call the local police department to advise them that we will be working in a certain area at a certain time. We give the police departments our license number, make and color of our vehicle and identify ourselves to them over the phone. At times police would ask us who we are following. We advised them were not able to discuss that. I also keep a Fraternal Order of Police sticker on my car so that officers know that I am a member.

In my business, as in most others, it is necessary to keep up with technology. I was keenly interested in the possibility of applying technology to surveillance. I bought a GPS/cell phone tracking system that made the job of following a suspect a whole new ballgame.

TRUCKING COMPANY INVESTIGATION

A trucking company asked me to help them investigate whether one of their drivers was violating company policy. They suspected that this driver was not following his designated route and was making suspicious unscheduled stops. I could spend my time following the driver, or I could apply technology to the job.

I attached a GPS/cell phone device to the driver's truck and returned to my office. The driver left the warehouse to start his day totally unaware that his route was being tracked electronically. I had a record of his whole trip, which I turned over to the client, and retrieved my GPS: case closed.

The News Herald's Timothy J. Gibbons did an article on my use of high-tech devices as follows.

High-tech private eye-Mentor sleuth stays hot on the trail of cases with assistance from computer.

"Move over, Sam Spade. Hang up your trench coat, put away the gum shoes (whatever they are) and stop packing the pistol. It's time to get computer literate. This is a boon to my business, Karl Lewkowski, president of Mentor-based Argus Investigations said looking at his computer screen.

On the fifteen-inch monitor, a little car was scurrying around the streets of downtown Mentor. The technology that goes into beaming that picture into Lewkowski's home office ties together cellular devices, satellites, and computer mapping software. The result: if it moves, we can find it, he said.

A private investigator who specializes in surveillance, Lewkowski has embraced the newest trend in high-tech people following: tracking vehicles by using global positioning satellites. With the owner's permission, Lewkowski can place a small device in a car. When the car moves, the device sends a signal to a satellite network which pinpoints its location. That information is then sent to a computer equipped with mapping software, which shows that the suspect car is driving down, say, Mentor Avenue.

We can tell where he is driving. We can tell how fast he is driving, the private investigator said.

Such an ability is beneficial when tracking cars in urban areas, where typical line-of-site surveillance is a little more difficult. With the GPS system, it doesn't matter if the suspect runs a red light; a laptop computer on the passenger seat can tell Lewkowski where to go when the light turns green.

Adding technology to his investigative toolbox made sense to Lewkowski, who has followed people all over the country since starting Argus six years ago.

In New York we followed a woman on foot for a week, he said—and then went on to recount adventures following people through Seattle, Texas, and Florida. Recently he spent some time following a person through the crowded streets of Mexico City.

Following people: that's what people pay me for, he said.

The article then goes on to describe other types of high-tech tools.

There were many other cases where I used the GPS to surveille a person for a client. The device, if I could install it on a suspect's car, made it easy to follow them in traffic, as I had my laptop computer installed on a shelf in my car. One investigator could perform surveillance without the risk of getting burned.

PHOTOGRAPHY AS A TOOL

One assignment we were hired to work involved a national price-fixing scheme. Our assignment required us to capture photographs of individuals who were present at a certain meeting so that others could identify them. The case lasted a little while, but we had one individual left to go, which was critical to the case. Normally when we were conducting a surveillance, we would call the local police department to advise them we will be in a certain area at a certain time. We did so on this case.

Well, the next morning as we drove to the area of the individual's house in a wealthy area of town, there was a police car in his driveway, so we left the area to watch from another position. I had a helper in the right seat with a camera ready as we observed our man pulling up to a stop sign. We pulled up alongside. Our subject's car had tinted windows, so my partner began yelling at him. The subject rolled down his window to see what we wanted, and we were able to get the final picture required by our client.

MISSING PERSONS

Finding missing persons was another core competency of Argus Investigations. Competency is essential, but luck seems to also play a role. We were sent to southern Ohio on a case to flocate a young girl. We were told that she would likely attend a country music festival called Jamboree in the Hills in southern Ohio. This jamboree drew approximately a hundred-thousand people and went on for days. We would need luck to find her in a crowd that large.

I had my PI intern with me who knew this girl and could identify her if we spotted her. When we arrived at the jamboree parking area, I wondered how we were going to find this girl among thousands of attendees. We parked our car and walked up to the entrance with our tickets to enter the festival. I was extremely skeptical of our ability to find our girl in this massive crowd of people.

My partner and I began walking around, but I felt it was hopeless. My partner's name was Dwayne, and as we were looking around, a voice shouted out in the distance, "Hey, Dwayne." We saw a girl waving at us far up on the hillside, and, lo and behold, it was the girl we were looking for. UNBELIEVABLE! We walked up the hillside and approached the girl who was with a group of others. We sat with them, chatted with them and enjoyed the festival for an hour or so. We also took pictures of us altogether at the festival. Our client was jubilant and thanked us for a job well done. Well, it was pure luck.

There were two missing person cases that I will never forget, as I believe God may have put me in the right spot to locate these two females. The first case was a family living on Cleveland's west side. They reported their daughter missing to the local police, and they were concerned for her safety. The police advised her to hire a PI, and they called me. I left my home office within a half hour and drove to meet with the clients.

The family gave me some ideas as to where she might be located. I took notes, asked the appropriate questions and left their home to begin my search for their missing girl.

Upon leaving the residence, I drove a short distance away and parked in a cemetery to review my notes and contact local agencies so that I might have more eyes looking for the girl. While reviewing my notes, I looked up, and, lo and behold, the young lady driving the vehicle that I was looking for came driving toward me in the cemetery lot. I waved at her to get her attention, and she stopped. I approached her car and told her who I was and that her parents were genuinely concerned about her. I talked to her for several more minutes when she agreed to go home. I followed her back to her house.

MISSING DEAF GIRL

The last case was somewhat like this one. I met with the family and learned that their missing daughter was deaf and could not speak. She was able to read lips. Their daughter was approximately twenty-eight years old and was probably heading to a Pennsylvania suburb. I left the client's home and started driving toward Pennsylvania.

After arriving in the general area where she might be, I found a restaurant and went in to get a cup of coffee to go. Behind the restaurant was a large parking lot that was nearly empty. I parked in the center of the lot, with no one around, and was drinking coffee and reviewing my notes when something made me look up at the driver's side window. The young lady I was looking for was standing next to my vehicle and preparing to put a poster of some sort on my windshield. For a moment I was in total shock and disbelief that I would see this young lady so quickly in the parking lot with no one else around. I looked at her and turned the inside lights on in my vehicle so she was able to see my lips. I told her who I was and how concerned her parents were that she had left home. Well, I was able to talk her into driving back home with me. During the drive, I would have to turn my inside lights on so she would be able to read my lips.

If the above two cases were not "divine intervention from above," I don't know what is. Soon after we drove away, I telephoned the parents to tell them that I would be driving their daughter home. They were obviously elated. End of another case!

THE CHICKEN CAPER

As you know from earlier chapters, I was in the retail grocery and meat business in my early years. That experience came in handy when I was asked to help a restaurant figure out where the chicken was "falling off the truck!" I thought I had experienced about every type of case imaginable, but this was a new one. My case report tells the story as follows:

On May 13 and May 15th, I conducted interviews with employees at the Southgate Mr. Chickenstore #1 per your request, as you had explained to me the shortages at this location. I spoke with sixteen employees during the two days I was there. As you had advised me earlier, we were dealing with mostly young people. I spoke with each individual and attempted to relate to them the seriousness of the piece count shortages of chicken. I assured each and every one of them that we would get to the root of the problem and solve the shortage situation. I did not expect any of them to tell me who they suspect is behind this problem, but most of the employees felt the drive through was the suspect area. Some of the people felt the second shift was the problem, as managers are mostly here on first shift. Some comments were: free chicken given at drive-through, management behind theft, possibly going out the back door, why not inventory before each shift, set people up to catch them, management should look in the kitchen more often, no night kitchen manager, monitor headsets, five pm to eleven pm has no one counting inventory, night shift problems with people cussing and fighting, too many packers and closers, they should switch off more often, drive-through should only take from their own trays, so this might solve the problem i.e. how many trays did drive-through use? How many did front people use?

Half of the employees I interviewed have been employed here a short time. Having seen a small part of the chicken business for two days, being a private investigator, former police supervisor, and having many years' experience in retail management, I can only give the following recommendations and opinions regarding the shortages in this Mr. Chicken store. The first topic I would address is the cameras which we have already discussed. The installation of a high-tech camera system would give the owners the upper edge in store supervision and control. I am of the opinion that adult supervision is needed at the Southgate store, especially on night shift. Are the chicken deliveries being weighed and counted each delivery by management? Having been in the meat business for many years, I am aware of the shortages that occur at the time the product is delivered. I understand that there is not a scale at the store to weigh the chickens. Is it necessary to check weight? Has the weight and piece count been accurate, or have you found shortages? As wings are a popular item, is there a policy in place as to who authorizes extra pieces to be placed in containers when the wings are small? Or when the breasts are small? Perhaps the shortages are occurring when the extra pieces are not calculated at the register? How are the pieces of chicken accounted for that are left overnight and frozen? Is there a miscalculation in this store as to the method of arriving at the high piece count shortages? Is the store showing a profit? I seem to be of the impression that actual money shortages are not occurring on a regular basis at this particular store. I am assuming that you use the same methods at all the other locations to verify piece counts. Please advise me of any change in that particular store since I interviewed the employees. I am looking forward to assisting you in any other concerns you may have. I am also looking forward to your decision to install the camera systems we discussed. Please advise me as soon as you can as we are ready for the installation process. I did not expect to solve all your problems at this store in the short time I was there, however, I hope I have instilled the fact in your people that we will catch the culprits.

Thank you,
Karl R. Lewkowski

EDDIE THE PORN GUY

Another interesting case requiring creative tactics was the case I will call "Eddie the Porn Guy." Eddie was in his mid-to-late twenties and was highly successful in whatever he was doing on the internet. I suspected he was involved with pornography and was, in my estimation, netting many thousands of dollars a month.

Eddie hired me to locate his wife who was traveling around the country with a small child to avoid being served court papers regarding the child. I was to find her and serve papers on her, requiring her to appear in court. I had no leads and was getting frustrated, but Eddie wanted me to continue no matter what it took. I was frustrated to the point I had to do something out of the ordinary to stop her.

The only lead I had was a PO Box address that I believed she used by having the post office forward mail to her wherever she stopped for any length of time. I mailed her a brochure and a letter identifying an introductory 800-number card that she could use in an emergency. If she used the 800-phone number, I would be notified of where the call had originated. I had bought this 800-number service online knowing that eventually it would come in handy. It was probably four to six weeks later when my fax machine went off late one night. I woke up and retrieved the fax that told me that Eddie's ex-wife had used the card. I was able to retrieve a good address in Colorado. I left immediately, along with an associate, to the address in Colorado.

We arrived at the address in Colorado early in the morning and initiated a stakeout from which we were able to watch her front door. My associate who was with me was behind the wheel of our rental car. We saw the female and the child leave the apartment and walk toward a vehicle. There was a man behind the wheel. I told my associate to block the car in its position so they could not leave while I served papers on the young lady. I exited our vehicle with papers in hand and approached the car. The young lady was in the passenger seat with a young girl. Her window was three quarters of the way down. I placed my arm with the papers in her hand and attempted to leave when the driver rolled up the window with my arm in it and began to drive away. My associate had failed to block the vehicle in which the young lady and child were in. I was being driven away with my arm inside the window of the vehicle! The vehicle was headed in a direction that would slam me into a telephone pole. I wrenched my arm free. If I were unable to free my arm, I would have been driven into the telephone pole. I was not too happy with my associate and let him know it. Eddie was elated, and the matter was closed.

SCOTTSDALE INVESTMENT FRAUD

It was mid-winter when I was hired to go to Scottsdale, Arizona, to locate an individual whom my client had trusted to invest quite a bit of money. I had several leads but with extremely limited information as to where this individual was located. I had a name of a woman who my client thought might be associated with our target. I got lucky and found a phone number for her and so made a pretext call. I pretended to be looking for our guy so that I could invest with him.

This worked, and she gave me his address. This happened within an hour and six minutes of starting this case.

I staked out his office from a restaurant where I could sit and have coffee while maintaining surveillance. He came out and I followed him to a secure condominium complex. I thought of a story to tell the person at the gate so that I could gain access to the condo. I told the person at the gate I was interested in purchasing one of the condos and was awaiting a real estate person. The guard let me in, and I was able to identify the subject's vehicle and his condominium.

I left the area and decided to go back for a photo of the target vehicle. I advised the guard on duty that I was just here with a real estate person and that I forgot to take a photo of the condo. Again, he let me in through the gate. I took more photos and left the area. I telephoned my client who was incredibly happy that I found out where this individual lived. Case closed!

ANTI-TERRORISM COURSE

Early in my time as a private investigator, I enrolled in a one-year special study at Ohio University labeled "Terrorism." The course increased my knowledge of terrorism to the extent that I was able to design a course that law enforcement and private security would benefit from attending. Prior to enrolling in this course, I was constantly on the computer and monitored worldwide terrorism tactics from terrorist acts committed in numerous countries. At the time I did not know how to utilize a database, so I printed out every incident of attacks that occurred throughout

Homland Security

the world. During study at home, I would perform more than the required wording of my assignments. I enjoyed the course immensely, which I believe made me a better-informed security person. I earned a Certificate in Homeland Security, Level Three from the American College of Forensic Examiners International.

In 1995 I gave a three-day class on terrorism to familiarize police and security professionals with the basic knowledge they required to understand the modern terrorist as they had become a force we must deal with. As the owner and chief investigator at my agency, many times this course of study proved invaluable to me in recognizing threats while conducting security surveys for business clients.

DEATH BED WEDDING

The Rock and Roll Hall of Fame had recently opened (September 1, 1995) when my brother and my two sisters all met together for the first time since we were split up as children. My brother, Tony, came all the way from Alaska for the reunion. Linda and I lived nearby, and Carol had come up from Florida. We had a great visit, including a trip to the recently opened Hall of Fame. We talked about our childhoods and told each other what we had experienced growing up without our real parents. It was rather strange for all of us to realize that we all had the same parents, and that we had actually lived together for a few short years. The girls, being the youngest, had no clear memories of early childhood, while Tony and I did have some memories. Now here we were, all with families of our own, and we were practically strangers. It was difficult to digest that we were actually siblings.

**Brothers and sisters reunited.
Karl (left) and Tony with
Linda (left) and Carol**

We all agreed that we would stay in touch, but that proved to be difficult with two of us living so far from the others and no real history together other than the few short years described earlier in the first chapter.

It was a couple of years later that I got word that Carol was deathly ill and in hospice care. Hospice care is available for seriously ill patients who are not expected to live more than six months or so.

I contacted my sister, Linda, and we agreed to both go to Florida to see Carol. Linda remembers this event as follows: "*When Karl and I went to see Carol in Florida, I felt strange staying with my brother for the first time in the hotel, but it was nice to get to know him some and to see our sister who was dying and to meet her kids. I always thought it was strange that all four of us had two kids each, a boy and a girl. Meeting them like this was quite depressing.*

"*We flew to Florida and stayed in a hotel near the hospice. Carol was bedridden and close to death. We met Carol's kids and her boyfriend, and much to our surprise, he and Carol were to be married at the hospice. The wedding was held while Carol was in the bed. The family decorated the room with flowers and decorations. The minister of the hospice nursing home performed the wedding service.*"

Bob, Carol's boyfriend, had always promised to marry Carol, but they kept putting it off. We were all overcome with emotion witnessing Carol being married on her deathbed. No one could witness this wedding without tears. Carol was surrounded by her own kids and her long-lost brother and sister. The hospice caregiver attended, and the ceremony was conducted by the hospice administrator.

Carol died shortly after the wedding in December of 1997.

EYE IN THE SKY

I investigated several cases where surveillance required unorthodox methods. These cases were critical in that we were required by the client to not fail on the first attempt and to not get burned. Using more than one vehicle would be required, and one of them would be an airplane. My friend, Ron Cola, owned a Cessna 150-150, and it was available for use as my "eye in the sky." A Cessna 150 is a two-place training aircraft, perfect for flying above the target with no chance of getting burned. The Cessna 150-150 had a 150 hp engine instead of the original 100 hp engine. I was once a flight instructor, so the Cessna 150 and I had spent many hours together. The only problem with this aircraft was that it has no toilet!

One such case began early one morning as we decided to be airborne at 7:30 am. The weather was perfect, the air was not turbulent, and the sun was shining. We departed on schedule and were over our target area at eight am flying a rectangular pattern waiting for our suspect. The small Cessna 150–150 was quite cramped with two large guys sitting side by side. I was able to see quite a distance with my binoculars and spotted our target vehicle approaching us from the south and I radioed my partner on the ground. We flew for approximately twenty minutes, keeping the vehicle in site always.

The suspect had no idea he was being followed. The suspect was driving as he had in the past, expecting to be followed, darting in and out of traffic, driving fast around turns, hills and valleys. We followed in the Cessna to a remote area in the country and observed the target vehicle park at a remote work site. We had completed our job in the air that we could not have done in a vehicle.

More pressing problems were evident as my bladder was full. I had drunk a cup of coffee prior to the flight and was desperate to relieve myself. I was in pain. I had to go *now*. I ordered my partner pilot to land the plane immediately. He had a small airfield in sight, and we both hoped we would make it in time. We did. I did my business on the runway and we were back in the air. Our suspect was still at the remote site. Our mission had been a success, and the client was pleased. Case closed.

INFIDELITY

Another case I recall was that of a man who hired us to follow his wife, as he had tried and failed. The client's wife worked at a large factory, and when work was finished at 4:30 pm, hundreds of vehicles would leave the plant. I attempted to follow her utilizing two vehicles, but it was impossible as we tried several times. The wife was aware of her husband following her on other occasions. I had access to a small airplane, so we followed her from the air. I gave instructions to our vehicle on the ground as we flew for approximately twenty miles to a hotel parking lot. Case closed.

BOUNTY HUNTING

Bounty hunting goes back to the days of the wild west when bad guys committed crimes and then escaped the posse riding off into the sunset. Sheriffs did not have the resources to pursue the miscreant, so they would issue "Wanted, Dead or Alive" posters with attractive rewards as an incentive to "bounty hunters" to capture the wanted. Today's bounty hunters are, for the most part, licensed professionals, many of whom are ex-law enforcement officers.

The following article from the News Herald, written by Dave Truman, best describes Argus Investigations work in this area.

More Respected Profession
Bond investigators praise new Ohio law to
regulate who can be bounty hunters.

"A recent change in Ohio law is helping one local private investigator drum up new business while cleaning up a dangerous industry glamorized by television.

For the past few months, bond investigators—commonly referred to as bounty hunters—

have been required to be licensed in the state.

In the past anyone could go after fugitives. Or bond skips, according to Karl R. Lewkowski, president and chief investigator of Argus Investigations Agency Inc. in Willoughby.

Lewkowski says he now has fifteen licensed bond agents continuously tracking down skips—a service that has become a growing part of his business.

Dan Shury, head of A-1 Bonding Agency in Willoughby, said the change in the law will help keep the cowboys out.

Lewkowski agreed. He said the most important thing to look for in a good investigator could be experience.

It's just like with a new lawyer practicing law, he said. Or if you want a heart surgeon, where would you go? You'd go to the best.

In the past, Lewkowski said, there were a lot of mistakes made. There was a lot of people doing it that shouldn't be doing it. A lot of police have a sour taste on bounty hunters.

Following paper trails, talking to snitches is nothing new to Lewkowski.

He founded Argus fifteen years ago after a long stint as a narcotics investigator in Alaska.

That experience comes in handy when Argus prepares to reclaim a skip or carry out any of its other operations in Ohio or elsewhere.

Lewkowski said having a good relationship with local police is important.

While private investigators can make arrests on their own, Argus calls police ahead of time to let them know when they will be in the area and the address of any potential arrest.

The people we're after are considered escaped prisoners.

Shury said he used to collar skips himself, but these days he leaves that up to "retrieval agents" such as Argus, or, in some cases, he simply contacts police to make an arrest when the subject's location is known.

According to Shury, the new law is a good thing for everyone involved.

Now you have a person that is responsible and licensed, he said. Every guy who watches TV and sees this type of thing thinks they are a bounty hunter. They think it's glamorous, but it is really hard work. You may sit and watch a guy's house for three or four days.

Lewkowski recently spent seventy-five hours in surveillance on Cleveland's west side for one case. He said many cases are broken by what is learned in a span of a few seconds after days of watching.

With probably half a million outstanding warrants in Ohio,

Lewkowski said he added ten to twelve new bond investigators to keep up with demand.

Each case could wrap up in a short time or drag out over several weeks and several states.

That's what Lewkowski relishes about the business. He said he never knows when the phone will ring and he'll hop on a plane to Mexico.

I love what I do or I wouldn't be here, he said."

INTERNATIONAL WORK

I received one of those late-night calls that surprised even me, who was getting used to unusual assignments. This client asked me to provide a team to travel to Tijuana and the San Ysidro area for an assignment estimated to take ten days. The requirement was to find and identify an individual. I was advised that other investigators had tried and failed. Within twenty-four hours me and an associate were on our way to San Ysidro. We were given brief information of where certain individuals who were known associates of our target might be staying. One of these individuals, I was informed, was a former government intelligence agent.

When we arrived at the motel where they were staying at, there was no one at the front desk, so I took the opportunity to look at the check-in sheet and found the rooms that our suspect people were occupying. When the clerk returned, I asked for a room near the people whom we were watching. We conducted surveillance on the individuals every day for several days. We had to cross the border, as they frequently went into Mexico. We reported to our client daily to update him on our progress. One evening, one of my partners and I were across from the motel in a wooded area watching the front of the motel. One of the subjects from the room, whom I believe was a doctor, left the room and began walking. We followed him on foot and saw him go behind an Arby's restaurant. There was the vehicle we were looking for and the individual that we were assigned to find.

I advised our client the date, time, vehicle, and description of the individual they were looking for. The client had only given me what information I needed to do our job.

We were finished with our case, and, on the way home, stopped in Las Vegas for a little entertainment before returning.

One of my clients whom I had worked for rewarded me with a trip to Israel. He asked if I would accompany him, as he was an elderly gentleman and did not feel comfortable going on the trip alone. It was the trip of a lifetime, and I have several hours of tape recording of my visit to Israel. It was a trip that I will never forget. We stayed at the Don Hotel in Tel Aviv. Our backyard was a beach on the Mediterranean where I went jogging every morning. During this trip, we met with quite a few military personnel and former military personnel while visiting in Israel. If I recall correctly, one of our drivers that we had was a former military officer.

ELECTRONIC TOOLS

I received a call from a former intelligence agent for a federal agency. He told me that he knew that his telephone was bugged. He had another investigator he had hired come to the house with a small black box piece of equipment who told him that his phones were *not* tapped. The client told me that he was an experienced intelligence agent and knew that his phone *was* tapped. We set up an appointment, and I arrived at his residence with our technical equipment. Within twenty minutes or so, we discovered a wiretap on the phone. He offered us a $20,000 bonus if we could locate the source of the wiretap.

Without going into detail, we could not locate the source of the tap. I later learned this client had been arrested and was spending some time in a federal prison. From prison he had called me to conduct another case for him on his spouse. I never heard from him again.

I recall another situation where I was conducting stationary surveillance and had my monitor receiver turned on. I intercepted a cellular call by accident that came over the airways. As I recall, the men talking were two federal agents who claimed to be on a surveillance in southern Ohio relating to a sniper case. It was hard to believe they were talking on the open airways about confidential matters. Having been in law enforcement in prior days, I would believe they would have a conversation or could have one using scrambled radios. As my memory recalled the conversation, they were also discussing a case whereby a confidential informant was going to be working shortly in the area and used names and the type of case. I was taping this conversation and forwarded it to the federal agency anonymously. Perhaps they might believe that I was a good guy and overheard the conversation knowing that it was quite possible that bad guys might also have heard the conversation.

I also came across a strange conversation that I had picked up by accident while on another surveillance sitting in my vehicle and monitoring my radio receiver. The call was between a man and a woman and is recreated from my recording.

The man was telling the woman that he gets into Langley all the time, the DefCon system! The male would not tell the female his handle, stating he could go to jail for a long time, as he had been doing this for four years. He said that he had quit a year and a half ago. The male talked about a Parma, Ohio, case several years ago involving Confidential Informant (CI) codes, and that he had rolled. I put him away. The male was talking to this female and referring to her new her husband's name by his code name. The male stated his systems are freak proof, and the female was discussing that the feds suspected Dan Krumlof of having ties with the West Germans. She also mentioned a Clifford Stahl. It sounds as if the female talking might work at the Improv, as she stated the line to the Improv was tapped. She questioned if the male Damon's was a fed? The female went on to say that Kevin plays dragons and dungeons with us. He's a four-hundred-pound albino, my best friend. She stated the feds are after him. They were trying to get him to pop some people. The female asks the male caller, "You're not a Fed, are you? Promise?"

I believe I sent the above to the FBI anonymously, as I still have an envelope marked with the notes.

CODE NAMES

There were three times in my private investigation career of almost eighteen years that I had used a code name when I would contact several clients that I had cases pending with. One case that I remember, I was working on the west side of Cleveland toward the Toledo area when I heard a call on my receiver of two investigators that were taking pictures of people entering a political function at a potential county commissioners house. They had described the house as they were talking to another individual, and I located the house and the address and found out who the owner was. I called the owner and advised him that my name was Martin and that I had information that he might benefit from. I advised him what was going on. He was thrilled that I called him and said he would send someone to investigate the matter. He could not have been more grateful and thanked me for the call. I told him if I ever needed a favor from him, I would call and use the name Martin. I never did call, but I felt I might have done him a good deed.

As a private investigator, I worked for a very well-known surgeon and was helping him to determine if his spouse was cheating on him. As he was a very well-known surgeon and quite busy, so he told me that he wanted all the information as soon as I found out what went on, so I would call him at the end of the surveillance, and the secretary would ask me who was calling, and I would say ABBASS. The doctor would answer the phone within thirty seconds of my call to him, and I would update him on what occurred that day. He was happy with the results.

The last time I used a code name was when I had a discussion with an individual from another country who was a member of that country's parliament. I had discussions with that gentleman in a prior meeting about a special assignment that they were interested in pursuing. I was highly referred to them as the person to be able to handle their situation. Somewhere I still have his phone number that I kept in case I had to call him for any reason; he told me to use the name Kaplan. He returned to his country, advised me that they had discussed it with other members of parliament and that they decided not to pursue the case. I might have mentioned this in an earlier column, but the two assignments that would have taken me out of the United States did not materialize. I was grateful to have such high referrals to both cases, but I believe when it came right down to it, I would not have accepted the assignments. I have worked one case in San Ysidro and Tijuana area and one case in Canada. I swore never to take a case outside the United States.

DAMSEL IN DISTRESS

An associate and I were waiting in my office where we were to meet a lady who thought that her house, vehicle and herself were "bugged" and sending her messages. The lady seemed very distraught, so I agreed to meet with her at my office. When she arrived, it was obvious she was not well. After calming her down, we began to discuss what she was hearing and the "signals" that she was receiving. We were both struggling to maintain a professional attitude toward her, as it appeared that she may have had a mental condition.

My associate began talking with the lady. He advised her to proceed to a grocery store and buy a large box of aluminum foil. He meticulously told her how to fold the foil starting at her feet, rolling it up her leg and around her entire body with the "sunny side up."

I was dumbfounded by what he had advised her to do, and I had to control my outbursts of laughter. We both maintained some sort of professionalism and advised the lady if her problem continued to see a psychiatrist. I did not have the heart to tell her that we could scan for the source of any type of electronic bugging using our equipment, but the price would be quite high. She seemed satisfied with our recommendations that if this problem continued to please see a doctor.

MY INTEGRITY IS QUESTIONED AGAIN: RUMBLINGS OF THINGS TO COME

During my career as a private investigator, I was questioned once about my integrity and honesty. I had to appear in court in the southern part of Ohio. My accuser, a former client, was claiming that I never called her or gave her information about the case that I was hired to do. The morning of the court case was the worst snowstorm I have encountered in quite a while. I drove the distance to the court, which was quite far, and arrived in court hours after leaving my office. The presiding judge was shocked when I told him I had driven down from Northern Ohio to be present for this case. I advised the judge that my integrity and my honesty were being questioned, and so it was important for me to be here. The client testified at the hearing that I did not advise her of the case and give her updates as needed. During my turn on the stand, I was asked by the judge to present my evidence. I showed the judge a lengthy report from my 800-call log that I had contacted the woman many times to advise her of my progress in her case. The case against me was dropped.

As the owner and chief investigator, I took pride in conducting the most difficult of cases. Clients would call and advise me that they had called previous investigators who could not complete their case. They were quite satisfied when I completed their case and found the information they required. I would soon get referrals from these clients that I had worked for, as they had friends that needed help and I was referred to them.

CLEVELAND INVESTIGATION

In mid-2000, I was serving a startup corporation in the Cleveland area. The company was genuinely concerned about security. I started conducting background checks for the president, who was in the process of hiring senior employees. I also drafted several security plans, including bomb threat and other crisis management plans. The president had purchased four secure phones through me for the executives in the corporation. I drafted instructions for how they should use these phones.

I toured the new offices, which were in the Cleveland area. We performed an electronic sweep of the new offices and premises in the downtown area. I happened to be excited about the new startup corporation, as I was under consideration for security director with a starting salary of $125,000 a year. I still have the four pages of an employment contract that was to be signed upon my being hired and having accepted the employment contract. As far as I recall, the new startup corporation did not receive the backup or the funding for the new corporation. I enjoyed working with this group and was proud of the fact that they had considered me for the position. I was disappointed but still had my investigative business, and life was good.

Debugging or TSCM was becoming an important part of my corporate security business. The following article from the News Herald describes this element of my business quite accurately.

Agency spies out bugs

Willoughby firm helps companies fend off espionage

With the corporate business world growing more competitive by the day, the threat of espionage rises as well.

"We're trying to make more people aware of the threat that is out there," said Karl R. Lewkowski, President and Chief Investigator for Argus Investigations Agency, Inc. of Willoughby.

Argus has been performing debugging procedures for years but says the past several months have seen a notable increase in the number of calls by customers who believe their security has been compromised.

Using technical surveillance counter measures (TSCM) sweeps, Lewkowski and his associates attempt to find the bugs.

The goal of TSCM is to located radio frequency devices as well as active or passive electronic devices and transmitters.

A company will call us and say, "We think someone is hearing our bids" or give some reason why they think they've been bugged, said Lewkowski, estimating the number of TSCM requests at about a dozen a month.

And, if we find a bug, we try to investigate who did it, he added. Finding those bugs can be a lot of work.

At times, we get companies with 20,000 square feet of office space, and it takes a long time to check all that, he said. If we find a signal, we may have to tear apart half the room to get to it.

He says targets of spying include companies involved in manufacturing, information systems and the environment.

Lewkowski adds a firm going through tough financial times, changes in leadership or looking to move could also be at risk.

And 99 percent of the time they are right, he said, adding the risk to him and his team rises when the client is a business. Companies have more at stake.

Bob Gelernter, an agent with Audiotel International Ltd., based in Corby, England, has spent the past couple of weeks training Lewkowski and his team on a new piece of surveillance equipment Argus has purchased. Gelernter says close to 90 percent of the companies in the United States have some sort of debugging system in place.

It's always been a big issue for them, Gelernter said of industrial espionage. Audiotel sells equipment to law enforcement agencies worldwide.

The Federal Bureau of Investigations estimates an annual loss of $24 billion in the United States from industrial espionage. It also causes millions of lost jobs.

Lewkowski founded Argus fourteen years ago after spending slightly more than a decade as a narcotics investigator in Alaska. The 1958 graduate of Riverside High School says becoming a private investigator is not easy.

We do a lot of work with high-emotion situations—life and death, he said. But I love my work, and if anyone asks, I tell them I have the best job in the world.

MIDDLE EASTERN FAMILY

A contact I had in New York had referred me to a middle eastern family who called me from Minnesota to discuss a case they needed help with. The complex nature of the discussion was such that I recommended that I meet with them in Minnesota. They agreed, and I flew to Minnesota to discuss their problems.

Upon landing at the Minnesota airport, I was met by a limousine with several middle eastern individuals, including a female. They drove me to a hotel in which I had a very luxurious suite. A large conference table was in the room. The discussion centered around a brother who was captured by Saddam's forces during the Iraq War. The family discussed hiring me to help them with this problem. I was advised by them that they were going to hire a mercenary, but that I came highly recommended. They discussed fees with me to manage the entire operation and to get help when needed. Apparently, money was no object. There was also another family included in this operation, which also had a family member in the same predicament. We discussed my fees, airfare, clothing, and accommodations while in the middle east. What contacts do we have now? What else would be in our favor? I was also advised by them that they had hired someone else prior to talking to me who apparently cheated them out of a large sum of money and did not come up with any results. In discussing my fees and questions I had, they all wanted a guarantee of positive results from me. The meeting lasted several hours, and I explained to them that if they hired the best attorney in the United States, I don't believe he could have promised a guarantee, and I would not lie to them to get the assignment. The bottom line was this: I felt honored that someone would refer me to such a task, but the thought of leaving my country and accepting an assignment in the Middle East was not my cup of tea. It was another experience as a private investigator that I will always remember. I always liked the most dangerous assignments, but in my own country, not overseas.

MY BROTHER'S STORY

My brother, Tony, visited me from Alaska, so I took him on a case or two with me to see what it was I did for a living. He wrote the following description of my job as a private investigator.

"The last time I visited my brother Karl, we spent an entire afternoon parked down the street from a dilapidated factory on Cleveland's east side. On the seat beside Karl lay his Colt .45 automatic pistol. The neighborhood was not a friendly one, and passersby eyed us malevolently. Binoculars sat on the dash above a laptop computer. The computer was mounted on a custom shelf that Karl had built for it in his old BMW. We sat in the car watching the factory for a certain white male to come out—our wait was five hours.

My brother is a private investigator, PI for short. Five hours to sit in a car was difficult for me but routine for Karl. The client in this case was a woman who had hired Karl to find out where her husband was staying. It seemed he had stopped coming home, and she suspected drugs played a role.

Around dusk the husband slipped out the backdoor of the factory, got in his car, and sped out of the lot heading east on Euclid Avenue. It was five pm, and rush hour traffic was picking up. We followed a short distance behind, and this is where I learned how much skill it takes to follow a suspect and not get burned. Our white male abruptly turned right into a parking lot next to a payphone leaving us no choice but to drive on by as if we had no interest in him. Traffic was heavy, but Karl smartly executed an illegal U-turn two blocks down, drawing rude salutations from other motorists, and headed back the way we had come. Another U-turn brought us smoothly to the curb within sight of and behind the suspect ready to resume the surveillance. Karl never broke a sweat, and I was impressed. The male made two such stops before speeding onto the freeway entrance heading east toward Mentor.

We followed, staying a few car lengths behind, being careful to keep some traffic between us. The chase grew intense as we maneuvered to maintain contact without being detected. as the suspect had the advantage—he knew where he was going, but we did not. Karl had some props handy on the rear seat in case we needed them. The props were items like hats used to alter some element of the picture the quarry would see in the rear-view mirror. An amazingly effective move made against discovery.

We were finally able to relax after our male exited the freeway in Mentor where he parked his car in the lot of a large apartment complex and went inside. We parked nearby for several uneventful hours until we were certain that he was settled in for the night.

Early the next morning we drove over and made a quick check to confirm the errant husband had indeed spent the night at the apartment complex; however, the case would not be closed until we were certain this was routine. Karl would check the next few mornings to see if the husband's car was regularly parked at the apartment complex. It was, and the client was given a detailed report. Case closed.

Effective surveillance is a skill that took Karl thousands of hours and seventeen years to perfect, mainly by conducting countless surveillance throughout the United States under different difficult circumstances. Surveillance requires patience, alertness, and a certain amount of creativity, along with a heavy dose of luck. Props are often used to alter the picture a suspect sees in his rear-view mirror during a moving surveillance and can include hats or other changes, or even more radical, a dummy that can be propped up to look like another person in the car. I stood in for the dummy during our recent case. In circumstances where losing the suspect would be disastrous to the case, or where the suspect may have to be followed for long periods of time, Karl will sometimes use a second car with another investigator to assist. The two investigators would stay in radio contact to coordinate movements between them. This tactic is used routinely when the suspect is criminally sophisticated or wary, requiring more advanced techniques and caution on the part of the PI.

Early one morning, while waiting for a suspect to start his day, Karl was in the process of acquiring a nondescript rental car in exchange for his BMW. The rental car was to arrive at eight am. The suspect unexpectedly decided to leave Cleveland at 7:30 am, forcing Karl to follow in the BMW. This surveillance lasted fifteen hours and covered a thousand miles, finally ending in Mississippi. Karl had to use extraordinary caution to keep from being discovered, especially during rest stops. Strong kidneys are critical in these situations.

I have grown used to my brother's chosen field of work. Even with his occasional strange requests. "If anyone calls your house and asks for Karl, just say that he lives here but that he is out of town just now," is one of my standing instructions. I did want to ask why. I often get calls from Karl when he is traveling on a case, sometimes at inconvenient times, but I listen regardless. He will give me a recap of the case which helps him think through his strategy while unwinding in some cheap motel room or expensive hotel, depending on the case. Following a wealthy suspect may require a room in the Ritz. While other cases may require less expensive digs. The client, however, always pays the expenses.

My brother is not the central casting version of a PI. He stands 5'6 and is almost as broad. He is extraordinarily strong from years of strength training and still very fast for his age. He was probably fast from his years of martial arts training. Karl spent about seven years as a police officer working his way up to a corporal. He has worked undercover drugs and served as a member of a SWAT team, which completes his resume of police experience.

Karl spent years studying terrorism before it became a national concern just because it interested him. His qualifying credentials for his work are extensive, and his personality suits his occupation.

Karl is a serious guy when it comes to completing a job for a client, but he also has a silly sense of humor that causes most who know him to smile when his name comes up. His version of the Three Stooges slapping his head while laughing loudly and whining is a trademark and especially funny as Karl somewhat resembles Larry. As you will see, a sense of humor is mandatory when your job requires you to deal with the underside of human nature daily. Who needs a PI for other than serious problems?

I sometimes envy his PI lifestyle, but I also wonder why anyone would do this work. The bread-and-butter of a PI's work is surveillance, watching a suspect from hours to days to confirm for the client that the suspect is performing some skullduggery that affects the client's well-being. Child custody, cheating spouse, workers' compensation fraud, theft of property, or trailing an employee. Sometimes surveillance can be eliminated by finding creative ways to catch a client in the act. Insurance companies often hire private investigators to gather evidence in cases where people claim they can no longer work due to an injury suffered on the job. Back injuries top the list of reasons that some people must retire with a benefit check. The PI's objective is to capture the suspect on film performing some task that proves that the suspect's health is fine for other activities but not for work.

One case proved difficult for Karl because he could not use the usual method, so he came up with a creative approach. The suspect lived in a rural environment and was giving horse riding lessons. There was no natural cover for my brother to use while waiting to capture the suspect in action. Karl made an appointment for a riding lesson for his young granddaughter. Naturally, being a proud grandfather, he brought his movie camera along to capture the young ladies' first ride. The action of the suspect stooping over to pick up a saddle and swing it onto the horse, followed by the granddaughter, provided enough evidence to the insurance company to prove that the suspect's back problem was no longer a factor prohibiting gainful employment.

Surveillance can be done other than sitting in a hot car if you use your wits. Creative surveillance can also be accomplished using technology. Karl had invested in some global positioning systems, GPS equipment, which coupled with cell phone and computer technology allows surveillance to be performed without leaving the office. A trucking company suspected a driver of not following his designated route but deviating for some purpose of his own, all at the trucking company's expense. Following a truck all day in traffic is not fun. Sitting home gathering the truck's position electronically and mapping this position every so often as Karl did proved effective and was more comfortable. This was made possible by attaching a GPS tracking device with cellular communications to the truck. The surveillance was done by calling the cell phone connected with a GPS and print out trucks position into mapping software. The trucking company received the evidence they needed to discipline the driver.

Domestic disputes and child custody cases make up a good percentage of cases for many PIs, and Karl is no exception. Surveillance is again the primary method of gathering evidence. Cases involving child abuse of any kind are always demoralizing by their nature, and the damaged spouse cannot usually afford the expense of a private investigator. Nevertheless, the proof is necessary to win a judgment in court. The PI is an effective way to gather and document evidence of wrongdoing.

Most of the PI's effort is not work that the police can do for you, as it is not their job. Private investigators are licensed by the state, and most are reputable and honest. However, care must be taken when selecting one to work your case. Be sure the PI you choose has a license and the required insurance. If your case requires surveillance, ask how much experience the PI has in this area. Check with the state agency governing PIs to see if there have been any disciplinary actions against him or her. Check with the Better Business Bureau for any major business complaints. Reputable PIs will cooperate with your efforts and provide references.

Suspicion of unfaithfulness causes people to react in ways that they normally would not. One older gentleman hired Karl to follow his blue-haired wife that the man believed was cheating. He would not be convinced that his wife went to the hairdresser, lunch with friends, church, and other innocent places. The old man gave Karl a pair of his wife's underpants to have analyzed for physical evidence of unfaithfulness. This proved too much for Karl, and he finally stop working with the old gentleman. The panty checks were popular for a while with the request for the service coming in several times a month. I once joked that maybe he should establish panty drops like the UPS and FedEx drop boxes to collect the garments.

Private investigations is a crazy business. Sometimes high-tech and sometimes low-tech is one of the contrasting elements of investigations. Occasionally clients hire my brother to debug their home or office premises with high-tech equipment to locate any bugs and/or to check the phone lines for recording devices. Physical searches are used to find hidden tape recorders. The client is always impressed when a bug is found, but this happens rarely. The client is usually satisfied if a bug is not found because they now feel safe in their activities. Just as the five year old feels better if you look under the bed and in the closet for the bogeyman. One CEO of a large company was watching as Karl performed a search of his office. The equipment picked up a very strong signal coming from the direction of the office window. But before Karl could confirm what the signal was, the CEO began ripping the drapery from the window, shouting I know it was here in my office. The signal had originated from a powerful commercial radio station located nearby, not from a hidden transmitter in the drapes.

Occasionally Karl will get a request to do something illegal. The client in some cases is not aware that what they are requesting is illegal. Sometimes they do not have any idea of what a PI does for a living. A PI with integrity supplements law enforcement agencies by performing work privately for a citizen that is outside the boundaries of what the police can do but nonetheless supports law and order. A reputable PI has a good understanding of the law and will not give legal advice to a client.

Dealing with people in distress can add a different dimension to the life of the PI. Many clients expect that surveillance must deliver satisfactory results, but sometimes it doesn't. The client may pay the investigator money for very little results. One client paid for a weekend surveillance in a campground, hoping to catch his ex-wife leaving their youngsters unattended while she partied with friends. Karl spent a very relaxing weekend at the campground as instructed, but the ex did not spend much time there as expected. The client would have been better served had he asked Karl to propose the most effective tactic rather than taking charge of the case himself.

Occasionally Karl got a very desirable assignment outside the norm. A wealthy client once asked Karl to accompany him on a trip to Israel with all expenses paid. Though not clearly stated, the client needed the company and probably wanted Karl along for security. The lifestyle is not for everyone, but for Karl it's a living. Sometimes routine, sometimes exciting, but always interesting."

Over the course of my career in private investigations, I conducted a variety of investigative and surveillance activities. Unfortunately, my case records were destroyed after I retired, so many of these stories are lost.

- Discovered union infiltrators in a nonunion shop.

- Major theft of goods by a supervisor and others in a city Housing Authority case.

- A case involving theft of $250,000.

- A month-long investigation utilizing covert cameras.

- A debugging case involving an owner and minority owner of a major sports team.

- A non-compete case involving preservation of evidence.

- Another case involving a corporate partner who was cheating other partners by billing time to himself and using company credit cards.

- An undercover case assignment in a large factory related to drugs and alcohol use.

- We conducted hundreds of marital infidelity cases.

- We also investigated a case whereby a person, a female in prison, was charged with negligent homicide, whereby the suspect in the case was already in prison for another case, having the same MO as the case the female was in prison for.

- As bounty hunters, we arrested several fugitives, returning them to their city of origin.

RETIREMENT

I am retired now and live in Mentor close to my children. I still maintain an intense interest in law enforcement and homeland security. The following pictures are of my many friends who served in law enforcement and government.

From left to right: former police chief Tom Fracci, Fred Piluso,
Former chief Jim McBride, State Representative John Rogers,
and Bob Phillips. From author's private collection.

From left to right: retired police lieutenant Ron Cola; Judge Mitrovich;
former Mentor police chief Tom Fracci; former police chief Mark Kish;
Karl Lewkowski; former police chief Jim McBride; State Representative
John Rogers; Fred Piluso. From author's private collection.

My brother and remaining sister are also both retired; we stay in touch and occasionally get together. Linda is retired from a career as a nurse and Tony from the telecommunication industry. Recently I got in touch with my deceased sister Carol's children and am planning on visiting them soon.

My childhood friend Tommy "Moose" Johnson died recently. I will always remember Mr. and Mrs. Johnson and their son Moose, who took me in and treated me as family. Rest in peace.

IN MEMORY OF DAVID BAKER'S DEATH IN AFGHANISTAN (2009)

On October 20, 2009, a major tragedy struck our family. My son's stepson, Lance Corporal David Baker, who was serving in the Marine Corps in Helmand province of southern Afghanistan, was killed. He had been a lifelong resident of Painesville Township. Since he was a young boy, he always called me Grandpa and my wife Grandma. Lance Corporal Baker served as a point man on his first tour in Afghanistan. Every father in this country would have been so proud to have him as a son.

David was on a foot patrol on October 20 when a hidden bomb exploded close enough to kill him. Helmand province was a Taliban stronghold area. In a phone call home, David had told his parents that he volunteered to be out front so that he could control the pace and be careful about others. Lance Corporal David Baker died a hero in everyone's eyes. He was a true

R.I.P. David Baker

Marine. Lance Corporal Baker was buried in Arlington Cemetery with many of the family members present. My wife and I also attended the service in Arlington. I must say, Lance Corporal David Baker was a true hero in my eyes who died valiantly for his country and saved my son's life.

My son was an alcoholic and has not had a drink since the day that David died, as my son realized what it meant to lose a family member and to live through that pain. It is now the year 2019, and my son has not had a drink since 2009. I know Lance Corporal Baker is in heaven, and I thank him and think of him often for saving my son's life.

EPILOGUE:
THE END OF AN ERA

TONI'S PASSING

WE CELEBRATED TONI'S BIRTHDAY ON February 13, 2016. She looked very frail and sad and said to me, "I will not make it to my next birthday." I asked her not to say something like that. I couldn't miss the pain in her eyes and her facial expression. It was so sad to see her in that condition on her birthday.

We celebrated her birthday quietly at home. During the evening of February 18, we watched television together. Toni arose from her chair and looked sadly at me and said, "I am tired and going to bed, Karl."

I said to Toni, "Would you like me to rub your back?"

She said, "No, I took a pain pill."

The next morning on the nineteenth as I was walking downstairs, I saw her slumped over on the floor in front of her chair. I ran to her side. Toni's skin was cold. I called 911 and told them of the situation. They asked me if I knew CPR, and I attempted CPR the best I could, but Toni was cold and gone. I was in total shock and called my daughter and son. Toni must have died very quickly, as I did not hear any noise at all upstairs in my bed. I believe I would have heard something, as I had done in the past but unfortunately I hadn't.

The county coroner came to the house told me that Toni had died approximately four hours ago. I sat with her until people from the funeral home came and took her there. I started to realize that my beloved Toni was gone. I do not remember much of the day after she was taken away. I just felt like my life was empty. I am so blessed that God decided to take her in that manner. She died at home, at peace and not in a nursing home or a hospice environment.

Toni had not been in good health for quite a while and was always hurting from her arthritis and migraine headaches. I now had to prepare for the funeral and burial in Mentor Cemetery. How many times had Toni and I visited the site of our burial place when we were at the cemetery and thought that both of us would be there someday? I cannot remember what I said at the funeral or how I felt because I can't even remember who was there. I also cannot remember who was at the grave site when Toni was buried. My mind was blank, as the most important person in my life was now gone forever.

Death is so final. I don't know what to say, but I will try to express my feelings in the best way I can, as I don't believe I can come up with the words as to how much she meant to me. I thank God for taking her in the manner that he did. Toni is now with her beloved family: mother, father, brothers and sisters who are together again. No one loved her family as much as Toni loved hers. Now, the only family I have ever known is all gone, including all seven children and the mother and father. I believe they are all together in heaven in peace. I can't explain in words how much love there was in my heart for my dear Toni. Even now, in 2020, as I write these words, I miss her dearly, even though it has been over three and a half years since Toni passed away. Sometimes, I must admit, it seems just like yesterday. I have always been a strong person and am very grateful to the Lord for taking her in the manner that he did and for giving me the strength to deal with her absence here on Earth. I thank Him daily and try not to be sad, but I just miss her.

All my experiences in this book have been written to the best of my memory and from my notes and other documentation. I am seventy-nine years old now and live alone in a small apartment near where I grew up. Since my beloved died just four short years ago, I have been carrying on but with a deep hole in my heart. I thank God for the time we had together and hold on to the belief that we will be together again someday.

My days consist of working out at my gym, visiting friends at the coffee shop, and helping care for my friend Chief Tom Fracci. Writing this book has been my main challenge, as I am not a professional writer.

Thank you, my brother Tony, for helping me get this book finished. My advisors tell me that this is probably enough information about me to publish now, but I plan to continue keeping notes so that I can add more material in my next edition of this book. I hope that all of you enjoyed reading the recollections of my life. I have been truly blessed by God and am grateful for every moment I have spent here on Earth and for every adventure found on these pages.

Thank you, Toni, for making this life worth living.

HEAVENLY CALL:
A POEM

BY KARL LEWKOWSKI

A call from heaven today
My heart pounding; I saw the word *Heaven* appear.
It rang as a choir of angels on my screen did appear
Even the ring sounded Heavenly to me.
I froze and thought, who would play such a joke,
how could this be?
Should I answer the call?
My heart pounding, my body shook.
As I touched the button, a heavenly voice said,
"Toni has tried out for the choir today and was accepted by all."
Each member is rewarded with a wish.
Toni wished this call to you, and the Lord agreed.
"Hello, honey," she said. "I love you and miss you too.
All is wonderful here in heaven.
My whole family is here; never been so happy,
specially to see Daddy.
We all love you and await your arrival.
When your time on Earth is over, we will be together again.
I know that my time is up now,
and I know you are strong and will survive the loneliness you feel.
Tell Bob, Connie and all the kids I love them.

All my love. Karl.
Goodbye for now."
I could not go to sleep the entire night after the call.
I had recorded it, but when I tried to play it back,
the call was silent.

Toni, my wife forever.
Family Photo

ABOUT THE AUTHOR

Commercial Pilot, Alaskan Cop/Metro Drug Unit and Commissioned Alaska State Trooper, Undercover Drug Agent, and Private Investigator.

Karl, after a difficult start in life, was orphaned at age six and married with child in 1957 at age sixteen. The marriage to his childhood sweetheart lasted for the next fifty-nine years until her death in 2016. Karl worked in the grocery business to support his young family while attending night school to earn a high school diploma. Karl then took up flying, earning a commercial pilot license. He worked as a charter pilot until he moved his family to Alaska where he became the oldest candidate at the Alaska police academy. He worked as a street cop in Juneau before returning to Ohio to work as an undercover drug agent, after which he went into business as a private investigator until retirement. He now lives alone near his son Bob and his daughter Connie. He has two granddaughters and five great grand kids.

ACKNOWLEDGMENTS

"**K**ARL, YOU SHOULD WRITE A book!"

Over the course of my adult life, I have heard that comment dozens, if not hundreds, of times, from friends, family, colleagues, and sometimes from complete strangers. But raising a family and working full time meant that that idea sat on the back burner for decades.

When I retired, I revisited the idea once again, and when my wife, Toni, passed away, this book became my primary mission. I also wrote it to leave a legacy for my family and friends, especially my grandchildren and great-grandchildren.

I'd like to thank the many people who encouraged me to write this book, especially my friend Jim McBride, who is the one who suggested the title *Cool Man Lewk*. After I told Jim that my best friends used to call me "Lewk," he said that I reminded him of Luke Jackson, Steve McQueen's character in *Cool Hand Luke*, the 1967 prison movie set in Florida.

My thanks also to Professor Robert Vaughn, Lakeland Community College retiree, who mentored me during this difficult project. A published author himself, he helps others in the community who wish to write their stories.

Thanks to my encouraging friends, who hang out at a local restaurant here in Mentor, Ohio, called Yours Truly. They include former Mentor police chief Thomas "Tom" Fracci, Fred Piluso (who owned the nightclub called Scruples, often featured in the original *Magnum PI* TV series), retired judge Paul Mitrovich, and my friend Bob Phillips. I also thank retired army major Bill Cardaman and Ohio State Representative John Rogers for their support and encouragement. I also want to mention Harley Badger and Frank Lewis, who supported my book project but sadly passed away while I was working on the manuscript.

I would also like to thank my brother Anthony "Tony" Lewkowski for all his help, without which, this book would not have gotten finished. Thank you, brother.

Last, I thank my little friend and companion Hero, who sat here with me night and day while I struggled with this work. He is living proof that dogs are, indeed, man's best friend.